How the British Invented Communism (And Blamed It on the Jews)

How the British Invented Communism (And Blamed It on the Jews)

RICHARD POE

First Edition, Second Printing, Second State
11 10 9 8 7 6 5 4 3 2
First Printing, May 14, 2024

Cover image by Ernst Sandau, 1913
Tsar Nicholas II and King George V, Berlin
(Image now in public domain)

ISBN: 979-8-9907510-0-2 (paperback)
ISBN: 979-8-9907510-1-9 (ebook)

DEDICATION

I dedicate this small historical correction to the memory of my Grandma and Grandpa, my father's parents, Pejza Lazarevna Burde and Rafail Aronovich Pogrebissky, in the hope that these words—long overdue—may help ease their final rest.

TABLE OF CONTENTS

FOREWORD

"Knowledge itself is power."

— Sir Francis Bacon

"If you know the enemy and know yourself, you need not fear the result of a hundred battles. If you know yourself but not the enemy, for every victory gained you will also suffer a defeat. If you know neither the enemy nor yourself, you will succumb in every battle."

—Sun Tzu, The Art of War

In 1991, the world was sold a lie. We were told that, with the USSR's "collapse", communism had lost. After decades of Cold War, this cruel and dehumanizing ideology would no longer be a threat. Nothing could have been further from the truth, for a new form of stealth communism was taking over the world under a new name: globalism.

When Klaus Schwab and his associates at the World Economic Forum tell us, "You will own nothing and be happy"—and when all our governments are rushing to implement Agenda 2030—it is hard to understand why we cheered when the Berlin Wall came down. What did we think we had won?

To fight globalism today, we must first take a new look at this thing called communism. What is it? Where did it come from? Why has this purported movement of the poor always attracted so much funding and support from wealthy elites?

Richard Poe has gone a long way toward answering these questions. In his new book, *How the British Invented Communism (And Blamed It on the Jews),* Richard argues that communism is a tool of the state, a psychological weapon developed by intelligence services, for the cynical purpose of subverting governments and controlling populations.

This thesis is supported, in Richard's book, by a wealth of fascinating historical examples spanning the Age of Revolution, from the Bavarian Illuminati of Adam Weishaupt to the Bolsheviks of Russia. Richard demonstrates convincingly that communism was largely an invention of the British secret services, who harvested ideas from early English socialists and weaponized them, transforming them into destructive ideologies suitable for dethroning monarchs and destabilizing nations. He reveals in great detail the hidden hand of British intelligence in nurturing and supporting both the Jacobin radicals who brought down King Louis XVI and the Bolsheviks who murdered the Tsar, effectively orchestrating two revolutions more than a century apart. Both could be described as early "color revolutions," that is, foreign-sponsored coups masquerading as spontaneous people's uprisings. Richard further explains why Lord Alfred Milner—the man most directly and personally responsible for bringing down the Tsar—praised socialism as the greatest secret weapon of the British Empire.

Perhaps most surprising is the strange alliance between Karl Marx and Scottish aristocrat David Urquhart, an arch-reactionary who sought a return to feudalism. What united both men, according to Richard, was their common disdain for the bourgeoisie. Both believed that the middle class constituted the greatest threat to a just and stable world order, and must be eliminated.

Fast forward to the present. The destructive policies of the Great Reset leave little doubt that the middle class is still the target, and that the unlikely connivance of Marx and Urquhart is very much alive. Thus communism, feudalism, and globalism continue their secret and incestuous affair to this day, giving birth to their monstrous progeny: the implementation of feudalism 2.0. Another vital ambition shared between them is the dissolution of the nation state. Since its inception, communism has always pushed "internationalism," and discouraged love of country. "I will conclude by wishing that the age may speedily arrive when there will be for all men but one country," said Karl Schapper, an early associate of Marx, at an 1846 speech in London, two years before the *Communist Manifesto* was published. And, of course, Marx and Friedrich Engels would drive the point home in their seminal treatise, by declaring, "Proletarians of all countries, unite!"

Looking at the world today, it is obvious that globalism is yet another psychological weapon like its predecessor communism. It is also clear that the architects of the "New World Order" are on the cusp of implementing their global communist system of governance. Centralized power and control over all the world's resources, including us, will be fully consolidated in the hands of the few. You and I will be relegated to a new, technologically-enabled serfdom.

As with all prior communist regimes, they will wipe out the intelligentsia. This time around, though, there will be no need to shoot people, as our brains are degenerating on their own through the misuse and overuse of technology, dumbed-down education, mass media indoctrination, and, before too long, degrading brain chips.

A caste of obedient minions are enforcing the new regime, led by the likes of Klaus Schwab and Bill Gates, following in the footsteps of Henry

Kissinger, David Rockefeller and other notorious agents of the New World Order, in an unbroken tradition going back at least two centuries.

Karl Marx himself was one such agent. But an agent of whom? Who are all these people working for? Who really runs this world?

Richard suggests that the demise of Europe's ancient aristocracy may have been exaggerated, and that many of the same princely families that ruled Europe for centuries may still be calling the shots, behind the scenes. Richard further suggests—and this is the point of his book—that the old aristocracy, especially in England, has made a persistent and systematic effort, through its intelligence and state propaganda services, to blame Jews for many of its own crimes and misdeeds, including the instigation of the French and Russian Revolutions.

As you will read in Richard's book, British War Secretary Winston Churchill in 1920 accused the Jews of masterminding not only the Russian Revolution, but "every subversive movement" in Europe for the past 150 years. In Richard's view, Churchill made this sensational charge in a calculated effort to deflect attention from a long history of subversive operations carried out by British intelligence. Richard writes: "To be clear, Churchill was not wrong when he said Jews were disproportionately represented in the Bolshevik movement. They were. But that was only half the story." The other half of the story, according to Richard, is that, "the Bolsheviks had no power to overthrow the Russian government nor to defeat the Russian military. Without British help, they could have done neither."

Why, then, did the British help them? We may never know the final answer. No matter how many layers of the onion we peel away, the truth remains hidden. But, with *How the British Invented Communism (And Blamed It on the Jews)*, Richard has managed to strip away more layers than most.

In the last few years, Richard has become a dear friend and trusted guide whose passion for lost and neglected history I share. Through his research and writings, he has enabled me and countless others to rediscover buried treasures from the past. Richard's brilliant new book goes far toward restoring some of the most important—and most forbidden—truths of our age.

It has been said that history does not repeat itself, yet it rhymes. Understanding the tricks our rulers have pulled on us in the past will help us recognize their deceptions in the present. Knowledge is power, said Francis Bacon. It is time now to reclaim our lost knowledge, and, with it, our power.

—Noor Bin Ladin

Acknowledgments

I give my deepest thanks to my wife Marie, whose love sustained me and whose wisdom guided me through every step of this journey.

Thanks also to Noor Bin Ladin, my dear friend, who helped me see the way.

To all those others whom I ought to thank, I thank you silently. The years have taught me that silence is golden.

Part I

Who Caused the Russian Revolution?

Chapter 1

Churchill Accuses the Jews

"THIS MOVEMENT AMONG the Jews is not new," wrote Winston Churchill. "From the days of ... Karl Marx, and down to Trotsky... this worldwide conspiracy for the overthrow of civilisation... has been steadily growing."[1]

Churchill was talking about communism. It was February 8, 1920. As Churchill wrote, all eyes were on Russia, where Bolsheviks and anti-Bolsheviks—"Reds" and "Whites"—were battling for control of the country. Before it was over, some 10 million people would die in the Russian Civil War, mostly civilians, and mostly from disease, famine, and mass atrocities on both sides. From this slaughter, the world's first communist state would emerge.[2]

Churchill blamed it all on a "worldwide conspiracy" of Jews. In a full-page article in London's *Illustrated Sunday Herald*, Churchill wrote: "There is no need to exaggerate the part played in the creation of Bolshevism and in the actual bringing about of the Russian Revolution by these international and for the most part atheistical Jews. ... [T]he majority of the leading figures are Jews. Moreover, the principal inspiration and driving power comes from the Jewish leaders. ... Litvinoff... Trotsky... Zinoviev... Radek—all Jews."

Churchill declared that the subversive role of "Jewish revolutionaries...

in proportion to their number in the population" was "astonishing," not only in Russia, but throughout Europe. These Jewish conspirators had now "gripped the Russian people by the hair of their heads," Churchill said. Unless something was done, many more nations would succumb to what he called "the schemes of the International Jews."

CHURCHILL SPOKE FOR THE BRITISH GOVERNMENT

Many readers will be surprised to hear such words from Churchill. We have been conditioned to think of him as the archnemesis of Hitler and the Nazis, a role he took on later in life. But, in 1920, Churchill's views—at least his public views—were hardly distinguishable from Hitler's.

As Secretary of War, Churchill spoke with the full authority of the British government. His article faithfully echoed Britain's official propaganda of the time. In April, 1919, the British Foreign Office had issued a report called the "Russia No. 1 White Paper: A Collection of Reports on Bolshevism in Russia," also known as the "Bolshevik Atrocity Bluebook." It identified Jews as the driving force behind the Tsar's murder and the Bolshevik Revolution.[3]

The British press followed up with a coordinated, anti-Jewish propaganda campaign, expressly promoting the *Protocols of the Learned Elders of Zion*, a document of dubious origin purporting to reveal a Jewish plot to enslave the world.

"EMBARRASSING BREADCRUMB TRAIL"

When *The Protocols* first appeared in Russia in 1903, they made little impact. However, British media now gave *The Protocols* new life, rolling out the first-ever British edition in February, 1920, under the title *The Jewish Peril: Protocols of the Learned Elders of Zion*.

The hand of the British government was evident in the publication of this book. The people involved in producing it left an "embarrassing breadcrumb trail to the door of the British Establishment," notes Alan Sarjeant in his 2021 study *The Protocols Matrix*.[4] Sarjeant concludes that the *Jewish Peril* was "part of a sophisticated propaganda offensive conceived and financed at the highest levels" of British power.[5]

The translators of *The Jewish Peril*, George Shanks and Edward G.G. Burdon, were military men with ties to Britain's war propaganda apparatus.[6] Its publisher, Eyre & Spottiswoode, was a respected government press entrusted with publishing the King James Bible, the Anglican Prayer Book, and other works owned by the Crown.[7] *The Jewish Peril*'s first press run of 30,000 copies exceeded that of F. Scott Fitzgerald's *The Great Gatsby* in 1925.[8]

According to Sarjeant, the promotional campaign for *The Jewish Peril* "was so professionally devised that practically all of Britain's national and regional newspapers had received a copy for review by the first week of February 1920"—that is, just in time for the splash created by Churchill's February 8 article.[9]

In the months ahead, leading British newspapers promoted *The Jewish Peril*. The London *Morning Post* ran a lengthy series of articles based on the book. "Read the startling revelations of what is causing the world's unrest. Read about the evil Jews' influence," ran a July 20, 1920 advertisement for the series.[10] *The Times* of London went so far as to question whether World War I had been fought against the wrong enemy. "Have we... escaped a 'Pax Germanica' only to fall into a 'Pax Judaica'?" asked a *Times* editorial of May 8, 1920.[11]

BLAME-SHIFTING

Why did the British establishment turn so suddenly on the Jews? I believe this was done to provide a scapegoat—a Jewish scapegoat—to deflect from British complicity in the Russian Revolution.

To be clear, Churchill was not wrong when he said Jews were disproportionately represented in the Bolshevik movement. They were. But that was only half the story.[12] The other half is that the Bolsheviks themselves were pawns in a larger game. A British game. And Churchill knew that.

In the interest of full disclosure, I should mention that my Grandma and Grandpa—my father's parents—were Jews, born and raised in the former Russian Empire. They lived through the horrors of the Russian Civil War, and were still experiencing those horrors when Churchill wrote his article in 1920. I cannot claim perfect objectivity in this matter. But I do think I can be fair.

I dedicate this small historical correction to the memory of my Grandma and Grandpa, Pejza Lazarevna Burde and Rafail Aronovich Pogrebissky, in the hope that these words—long overdue—may help ease their final rest.

CHAPTER 2

LEON TROTSKY, BRITISH AGENT

THE REALITY IS that the Bolsheviks had no power to overthrow the Russian government nor to defeat the Russian military. Without British help, they could have done neither. Of all the dirty secrets of the Russian Revolution, this may be the dirtiest.

Our story begins with Leon Trotsky. It was Trotsky who directed the Bolshevik coup of November 7, 1917, and Trotsky who led the Red Army to victory in the Russian Civil War. Without Trotsky, there would have been no Soviet Union. But Trotsky did not accomplish these feats on his own. He had help from the British government. Trotsky's longstanding ties to British intelligence have never been adequately explained.

TROTSKY AND BRITISH INTELLIGENCE

When the Tsar was overthrown on March 15, 1917, Trotsky was working as a journalist in New York City. He set sail for Russia, but British authorities arrested him when his ship stopped in Halifax, Nova Scotia. The British held Trotsky for a month in a Canadian internment camp.

For reasons unknown, the British secret service came to Trotsky's rescue, ordering his release. The order came from William Wiseman,

US station chief for Britain's foreign intelligence division, later known as MI6.[13] Following Trotsky's release on April 29, 1917, he embarked for Russia and joined the Revolution. The rest is history.[14]

In Russia, British handlers kept Trotsky close. One of his handlers was Clare Sheridan, who happened to be Winston Churchill's first cousin. She was a sculptress who claimed to be a Bolshevik sympathizer. Sheridan sculpted Trotsky's portrait, and was rumored to be his lover.[15] Reliable sources have identified Sheridan as a British spy.[16]

Trotsky was banished by Stalin in 1929, spending the rest of his life on the run. During the Moscow Treason Trials of 1936-1938, Trotsky was convicted, in absentia, of working for Britain's Secret Intelligence Service (SIS). The star witness against him was Soviet diplomat Christian Rakovsky, who testified that British intelligence had blackmailed him in London in 1924, using a forged letter, all allegedly with Trotsky's knowledge and approval. "I went to Moscow and talked to Trotsky [afterwards]," Rakovsky testified. "Trotsky said that the forged letter was only an excuse. He agreed that we were to work with the British Intelligence."[17]

HIDDEN HISTORY

Soviet show trials are not the most reliable sources. However, a good deal of independent evidence corroborates Rakovsky's testimony. If Rakovsky's charge is true, then Trotsky was already working for British intelligence in 1924. Some evidence suggests that British handlers may have been grooming Trotsky as early as 1902.[18] He was plainly receiving special courtesies from Britain's secret services in 1917, when MI6 mysteriously freed Trotsky from a Canadian internment camp. For all these reasons, it seems reasonable to conclude that Trotsky was a British asset—and probably a trusted asset of long standing—in February, 1920, when Churchill decided to publicly denounce him as a scheming "International Jew."

Seen in this light, Churchill's anti-Jewish rant in the *Illustrated Sunday Herald* begins to look like play-acting, like the spinning of an elaborate yarn, a cover story. But covering for what? What was Churchill trying to hide, by blaming Jews—and Trotsky, in particular—for the Russian Revolution? You will not find the answer in conventional history books. The story has been erased. But, in 1920, memories were still fresh. Witnesses were speaking out. The British faced hard questions about their role in the Russian Revolution. They needed a scapegoat.

CHAPTER 3

BETRAYING THE
RUSSIAN ROYALS

S IR GEORGE BUCHANAN, who was British ambassador to Russia from
1910 to 1918, would devote 16 pages of his 1923 memoir to denying
that Great Britain had orchestrated the Russian Revolution.[19] Why did he
need to deny this?

The reason is that prominent Russian exiles were accusing Britain
of complicity in the Revolution, among them Princess Olga Paley (pronounced pah-LAY), widow of the Tsar's uncle Grand Duke Paul. Paul was
the brother of Tsar Alexander III, Nicholas II's father. In the June 1, 1922
Revue de Paris, Princess Paley wrote:

> "The English Embassy, on orders from [Prime Minister] Lloyd
> George, had become a hotbed of propaganda. The Liberals, Prince
> Lvoff, Miliukoff, Rodzianko, Maklakoff, Guchkoff, etc., met there
> constantly. It was at the English Embassy that it was decided to
> abandon the legal ways and embark on the path of the Revolution."[20]

The Princess likewise accused French ambassador Maurice Paléologue of assisting Buchanan in these intrigues, albeit reluctantly. "His position at this period was very delicate," she wrote. "He [Paléologue] was getting from Paris the most definite orders to support in everything the policy of his English colleague, and yet he realized that this policy was contrary to the interests of France."[21]

FRANCE SUBSERVIENT TO ENGLAND

Paléologue admits, in his own 1925 memoir, that Buchanan's collusion with Russian radicals often put the French embassy in an awkward position. "I have been questioned several times about Buchanan's relations with the liberal parties, and actually asked in all seriousness if he is not secretly working for a revolution," writes Paléologue in an entry dated December 28, 1916.[22]

Paléologue routinely denied such charges, insisting that Buchanan was a "perfect gentleman" who "would think it an utter disgrace to intrigue against a sovereign to whose court he is accredited." In response, a certain Prince Viazemsky once gave Paléologue a "challenging glance" and retorted, "But if his Government has ordered him to encourage our anarchists, he is obliged to do so!" Paléologue countered, "If his Government ordered him to steal a fork the next time he dines with the Emperor, do you think he would obey?"

Paléologue doubtless understood that, if ordered to do so, his British colleague would not only steal a fork, but every last stick of the Tsar's silverware. Nonetheless, with nearly 3 million German troops inching toward Paris, France depended on Britain for her very survival, and was in no position to rock the boat.

KNOWLEDGE OF BRITISH PLANS

When Princess Paley identified the British Embassy as the nerve center of the Revolution, she was not just passing along gossip. She had inside knowledge of British operations in St. Petersburg (or Petrograd, as it was renamed in 1914). Her husband Grand Duke Paul was deeply involved in the intrigues leading up to the Tsar's abdication. At every step, he and his royal relatives worked closely with the British Embassy.

His son Dmitri (the Princess's stepson) was also caught up in British plots. On December 30, 1916, Dmitri took part in the assassination of the "mad monk" Rasputin. For a hundred years, historians have told us this operation was led by Prince Felix Yusupov—a gay, cross-dressing socialite—but all evidence suggests that the real leader was Lieutenant Oswald Rayner, a British intelligence operative who had been Yusupov's close friend at Oxford.

Rayner was present at the murder scene and is believed to have fired the fatal bullet into Rasputin's head, according to Andrew Cook's *To Kill Rasputin* (2006).[23] According to Cook, a secret British communication confirmed the killing, stating, "our objective has clearly been achieved. Reaction to the demise of 'Dark Forces' has been well-received by all… Rayner is attending to loose ends." "Dark Forces" was British code for Rasputin and his cabal of "reactionary" followers at the Russian court.[24]

We can thus see that Princess Paley and her family had rendered many services to the British Crown, even to the point of deceiving their own Sovereign. Despite these services, the Princess and her family were betrayed and abandoned by the British, as indeed all of Russia was betrayed.

Russian liberals like the Grand Duke Paul had been led to believe that Britain would help them establish an enlightened constitutional monarchy in Russia, run on democratic principles. Instead, Russia got five years of civil war, followed by 70 years of Communist rule. In the end, Princess Paley's husband and her only son were murdered by the Bolsheviks, her husband shot, her son Vladimir thrown down a coal shaft and crushed by logs and stones.[25]

STRANGE ALLIANCE

"A strange ally, Great Britain," the Princess mused in her 1924 autobiography *Memories of Russia 1916-1919*.[26] In her book, the Princess wonders how Russians could have been fooled into trusting the British, "for, in the history of Russia," she writes, "the animosity of England traces a red line across three centuries."

She was right. The Princess correctly notes that Britain struggled for 300 years to stop Russia from attaining what she calls a "free sea" (by which she meant access to warm-water ports). Much blood had been spilled over this.

Bolshevism, the Princess suggests, was just one more weapon deployed by the British to keep Russia weak. "Is it not to Great Britain that we owe the continuation of the Russian agony?" she asked. "Great Britain supports wittingly… the Government of the Soviets, so as not to allow the real Russia, the National Russia, to come to life again and raise itself up." All evidence suggests that Princess Paley was right. The Bolsheviks were indeed pawns in a British chess game.

Part II

Britain's 300-Year Blood Feud with Russia

CHAPTER 4

OLD RIVALS

E VER SINCE RUSSIA'S first emergence as a world power during the 17th century, British statesmen had regarded the Slavic empire with suspicion. They foresaw that Russia might one day prove an obstacle to England's ambitions in the East.

Britain's antagonism toward Russia persisted through World War I. In the Great War, Britain and Russia were technically allies, but the British believed they had more to gain if Russia lost than if she won. This is yet another dirty secret underlying many mysteries of the Russian Revolution.

In 1915, the Russians were in full retreat, taking heavy losses. The Germans, Austrians, and Turks were advancing on three fronts. Germany offered Russia a separate peace. Tsar Nicholas was tempted to accept.[27] The Allies could not permit that. So they made Tsar Nicholas an offer he couldn't refuse. In March, 1915, the Allies concluded a secret pact with the Tsar, promising to give him Constantinople and the Dardanelles, in the event of an Allied victory. The only condition was that Russia must stay in the war and fight to the bitter end.[28]

Russia accepted these terms. But subsequent events make clear that the British never intended to keep their promise. As Princess Paley noted, keeping Russia out of the Mediterranean was a centuries-old British policy. If Russia were allowed to take the Dardanelles now, her warships could challenge British control of the Suez Canal and the trade routes to the East. No British government in 1915 would have allowed that.

RUSSIAN DEFEAT—A BRITISH WAR GOAL?

In her memoir, Princess Paley states that British Prime Minister Lloyd George, "on hearing of the fall of Tsarism in Russia, rubbed his hands together, saying, 'One of England's war-aims has been attained!'"[29] The Princess does not name her source, and the quote is likely apocryphal. Nonetheless, the story reveals the suspicion many Russians felt regarding England's hidden motives. Some evidence suggests that British leaders really did hope and plan for the defeat of their Russian ally, from the very outset of the war.

This was certainly the attitude of Lord Herbert Kitchener, who served as Secretary of War from August 5, 1914 to his death on June 5, 1916. In his 1989 book *A Peace to End All Peace*, US historian David Fromkin notes that Lord Kitchener viewed Russia as a permanent enemy, the only European power capable of challenging British supremacy in Asia. Fromkin writes:

"In Kitchener's view, Germany was an enemy in Europe and Russia was an enemy in Asia: the paradox of the 1914 war in which Britain and Russia were allied was that by winning in Europe, Britain risked losing in Asia. *The only completely satisfactory outcome of the war, from Kitchener's point of view, was for Germany to lose it without Russia winning it* [emphasis added]—and in 1914 it was not clear how that could be accomplished."[30]

As it happens, the British managed to achieve precisely the result Kitchener sought. Germany lost the war, but Russia failed to win it.

CHAPTER 5

THE GREAT GAME

THE BRITISH HAD long experience outwitting and outfoxing Russia. They called it the Great Game. British intelligence officer Arthur Conolly is said to have coined the term "Great Game" in 1840, to describe the intricate, spy-vs.-spy maneuvers of British and Russian agents vying for advantage in the wastes of Central Asia, as Britain tried desperately to slow Russia's advance toward India.[31] However, the Great Game was not just about India, nor did it begin in 1840. It had been going on for centuries.

When English explorers first made contact with Russia in 1553, they found a weak, isolated realm, struggling to drive out the last of the Asiatic warlords who had conquered Russia 300 years earlier. Mongol and Tatar princes still held the Black Sea coast in 1553, just as they had since the days of Genghis Khan. But now they were vassals of Suleiman the Magnificent, the Turkish Sultan. Russia's southern coast was under Turkish control. Russian ships could not sail the Black Sea without the Sultan's permission.

Tsar Ivan IV—known as Ivan the Terrible—welcomed the British traders, at first, but became angry when they demanded a monopoly over Russian trade. For their impudence, Ivan expelled the newly-established British Muscovy Company.[32]

WHY ENGLAND BACKED THE TURKS

Two hundred years later, Russia was no longer weak. The Russian Empress Catherine the Great had finally succeeded in expelling the Turks from the Black Sea shore, after fighting two wars with the Sultan (1768-1774 and 1787-1792).

Catherine's success set off alarm bells in London. The Russians now had seaports on the Black Sea, threatening British control of the Mediterranean. When the Black Sea fortress of Ochakov fell to Russian forces in 1788, the English threatened war, demanding that Catherine return the fortress to the Sultan. She refused. The British backed down, dropping their ultimatum, but vowed to stop further Russian expansion.[33]

Their strategy was to play off Muslim against Christian. For the next hundred years, the British propped up the faltering Ottoman Empire, as a counterweight, to keep Russia in check. Their plan was to keep Muslims and Christians locked in a permanent stalemate or "balance of power," a never-ending conflict which neither side could win.[34] Both powers would thus be neutralized, leaving the British free to do as they pleased in the Eastern Mediterranean.

THE "GREEK PLAN"

Catherine's strategy was the opposite of the British. Instead of pitting Muslim against Christian in a permanent "balance of power," Catherine sought to unite Christians in a common cause, to drive the Turks out of Europe. The Ottomans still ruled a large part of Europe, including Greece and the Balkan nations of Bulgaria, Romania, Serbia, Albania, Moldova, Kosovo and Macedonia. Catherine's plan was to liberate these Christian lands from Muslim rule.

She sought to restore the Byzantine Empire, under the Greek Orthodox faith. Her grandson Constantine would be crowned Byzantine Emperor. His capital would be in Constantinople (which Russians affectionately called Tsargrad, City of Caesar). Catherine called this her "Greek Plan" (*Grechesky proyekt*).[35]

RUSSIA'S BYZANTINE ROOTS

Catherine's nostalgia for the Byzantine Empire had deep roots in Russian history. It was the Byzantines who had Christianized Russia during the Dark Ages and invented an alphabet for the illiterate Slavs. The friendship between Greek and Slav never faded.

Prior to 988 AD, the Eastern Slavs (ancestors of the Russians, Ukrainians and Belarusians) were pagans, worshipping the old Slavic gods. Vladimir the Great, Grand Duke of Kiev, converted to Christianity in 988, embracing the Eastern Orthodox faith of the Byzantine Greeks. Byzantine missionaries devised an alphabet for the Slavs, based on the Greek alphabet, the basis of today's Cyrillic writing system.

When Constantinople fell to the Turks in 1453, many Byzantines fled to Russia, where they were warmly welcomed. The Grand Prince of Moscow, Ivan III, married the Byzantine princess Sophia Paleologa, niece of the last Byzantine emperor. Her uncle, the Emperor Constantine XI Palaiologos, had died fighting the Turks in the streets of Constantinople.

In honor of the fallen Byzantine Empire, Ivan adopted the Byzantine double-headed eagle as Russia's coat-of-arms. He gave himself the title "Tsar" (meaning Caesar) and declared Moscow the "Third Rome," successor of the "Second Rome," Constantinople, now in Turkish hands. Thus was the Russian Empire born, like a phoenix, from the ashes of Constantinople.[36] For these reasons, a bond has long existed between

Russia and Greece. The Russians look to Byzantium as their spiritual ancestor, while the Greeks look to Russia as savior and protector.

WHY ENGLAND OPPOSED THE "GREEK PLAN"

Catherine hoped that her so-called "Greek Plan" would appeal to Christian rulers, be they Catholic or Orthodox. She secretly proposed it to the Holy Roman Emperor Joseph II in 1780.[37] However, the British had other ideas. They soon learned of Catherine's plan and resolved to stop it. The British understood that Catherine's new Byzantine Empire would be a faithful ally of Russia, sharing the same Orthodox faith. It would completely replace the old Ottoman Empire, tipping the power balance in Russia's favor.

In that event, the British would no longer be able to play off Turks against Russians, Muslims against Christians. They would face a united front of Orthodox Christians, guarding the gateways to the East. Even worse for the British, Catherine's new Byzantine Empire would open the Dardanelles to Russia, giving Russian warships access to the Mediterranean. Britain would lose control of the Mediterranean and the trade routes to the East. For these reasons, the British resolved to defeat Catherine's plan.

CHAPTER 6

"DOMINION OF THE WORLD"

CATHERINE THE GREAT died in 1796, but her Greek Plan lived on. England's opposition to the Greek Plan would ultimately lead to the Russian Revolution.

Throughout the 19th century, British strategists pondered how to keep Russia from taking Constantinople and the Dardanelle Straits. They called it the "Eastern Question." Unfortunately for the British, their Turkish ally was growing weaker while the Russians grew stronger. The Ottoman Empire was in long-term decline. And so the British did a delicate dance, playing off Russian against Turk, Turk against Russian, as the occasion demanded, often switching sides with dizzying suddenness.

Thus, when the Russians instigated a Greek rebellion against the Turks in 1821, the British betrayed their Turkish allies and sided with the Greeks. By this means, the British won the friendship of the new Greek state, and prevented Greece from becoming a Russian dependency.[38]

On the other hand, when the Russians attacked the Turks in 1853, the British sided with the Sultan. French and British armies invaded Russia, defeating her in the Crimean War of 1853-1856. The peace terms of the Crimean War required Russia to demilitarize the Black Sea. An angry, humiliated Tsar Alexander II was forced to disperse his Black Sea Fleet and destroy his fortifications.[39]

WHO WILL RULE THE WORLD?

British strategists of the Victorian era believed the "Eastern Question" would one day determine who ruled the world. In their quest for global dominion, they saw Russia as their chief rival. As David Fromkin puts it in his aforementioned book *A Peace to End All Peace*:

> "Defeating Russian designs in Asia emerged as the obsessive goal of generations of British civilian and military officials. Their attempt to do so was, for them, 'the Great Game,' in which the stakes ran high. George Curzon, the future Viceroy of India, defined the stakes clearly: 'Turkestan, Afghanistan, Transcaspia, Persia… they are the pieces on a chessboard upon which is being played out a game for the *dominion of the world*.' Queen Victoria put it even more clearly: it was, she said, 'a question of Russian or British supremacy in the world.'"[40]

Queen Victoria took the Great Game very seriously, and was determined to prevail, as her correspondence with Prime Minister Benjamin Disraeli reveals.

"PEOPLE WHO HARDLY DESERVE THE NAME OF REAL CHRISTIANS"

During the so-called Great Eastern Crisis of 1875-1878, Christian populations rose up in revolt throughout the Ottoman Empire. The Turks suppressed these risings with startling cruelty, slaughtering Christians by the tens of thousands. In Bulgaria alone, as many as 100,000 Christians may have been killed.

Europeans were outraged. At least, most of them were. Queen Victoria, however, defended the Turks. "It is not the question of upholding Turkey: it is the question of Russian or British supremacy in the world!" she explained in a letter to Disraeli on April 19, 1877.[41] In Victoria's view, the only thing that mattered was keeping the Russians out of Constantinople. If that meant abandoning eastern Christians to genocide, so be it.

Russia, on the other hand, decided to rescue the beleaguered Christians, declaring war on the Ottomans on April 24, 1877. A Russian army invaded the Ottoman Empire, marching through Romania and Bulgaria (both under Turkish rule at the time) and advancing on Constantinople.

Queen Victoria wanted the Russians stopped. As for the poor, suffering Christians, they were mostly Eastern Orthodox. Who cared about them anyway? "This mawkish sentimentality for people who hardly deserve the name of real Christians… is really incomprehensible," Victoria wrote Disraeli on March 21, 1877.[42] The eastern Christians were "quite as cruel as the Turks," Victoria stated on June 27. "Russia is as barbarous and tyrannical as the Turks," she added.[43]

VICTORIA'S WRATH

As the Russians advanced on Constantinople, Victoria's letters to Disraeli grew increasingly frantic. Referring to herself in the third person, in accordance with the royal custom of the day, Victoria demanded military action, repeatedly threatening to abdicate if Constantinople fell.

"Russia is advancing and will be before Constantinople in no time!" she wrote on June 27. "Then the government will be fearfully blamed and the Queen so humiliated that she thinks she would abdicate at once. Be bold!"[44]

On January 10, 1878, Victoria wrote Disraeli that she could not bear the shame of allowing England to "kiss the feet of the great barbarians [the Russians], the retarders of all liberty and civilisation that exists… Oh, if the Queen were a man, she would like to go and give those Russians, whose word one cannot believe, such a beating!"[45]

Only ten days later, Victoria got her wish. As the Russians reached the outskirts of Constantinople, the British finally intervened. They warned the Russians to halt, sending a fleet of warships through the Dardanelles to protect the Turkish capital.

Fearful of the British fleet, the Russian army came to a halt at the village of San Stefano, on January 20, 1878, only seven miles from the center of Constantinople.[46] This was the closest the Russians ever got to their dream of a New Byzantium.

KEEPING RUSSIA IN THE WAR

Britain's obsession with the "Eastern Question" remained undiminished at the outset of World War I. British statesmen were just as determined as ever to keep Russia out of the Straits.

But the situation had changed. The Ottoman Empire was now at war with England. The Turks had made an alliance with Germany on August 2, 1914. In addition, Russia's situation had changed. The Russian army was showing unexpected weakness. In the first month of war, the Germans annihilated two Russian armies, killing as many as 120,000 men. The Germans offered Russia a separate peace, and the Russians were listening.[47] Britain scrambled to help her faltering ally, frantic to keep Russia in the war.

On January 1, 1915, Russian commander-in-chief Grand Duke Nicholas (a cousin of the Tsar) requested help from the British. The Turks were hitting the Russians hard in the Caucasus. The Grand Duke asked the British to attack the Ottomans in the West, to relieve pressure on Russian troops in the East.[48] The British agreed. They had no choice. If they refused to help, the Russians would make a separate peace with the Central Powers. Thus began one of the strangest, most mysterious episodes of World War I—the Gallipoli Campaign.

CHAPTER 7

THE RIDDLE OF GALLIPOLI

I N RESPONSE TO the Russian request, the British promised a direct attack on the Dardanelles. If the attack were successful, Constantinople would fall, and the Ottoman Empire with it. But the attack failed. Catastrophically.[49] Military historians have spent more than a hundred years trying to figure out why.

On March 18, 1915, an Anglo-French fleet sailed up the narrow, 38-mile Dardanelles channel toward Constantinople. But they were turned back with heavy losses from mines and artillery fire. On April 25, the Allies tried again, this time with an amphibious assault on the Gallipoli Peninsula (which forms the northern shore of the Straits).

Over an eight-month period, more than 410,000 British and Commonwealth troops—including British, Irish, Australians, New Zealanders, and Indians—would land on the Gallipoli beaches. Nearly 47,000 would die. About 79,000 French troops also took part in the attack, of whom 9,798 were killed, bringing the total Allied dead to 56,707.

In the end, the attack was abandoned. Allied troops were withdrawn between December 7, 1915 and January 9, 1916. Winston Churchill was blamed, perhaps unjustly. He was forced to step down as First Lord of the Admiralty.

BUNGLING OR SUBTERFUGE?

Most historians blame the Gallipoli disaster on recklessness and incompetence. However, some suggest that the British deliberately pulled their punches, allowing the Turks to win. One such is Harvey Broadbent, an Australian historian who has written four books on the Gallipoli Campaign, including *The Boys Who Came Home* (1990), *Gallipoli: The Fatal Shore* (2005), *Defending Gallipoli* (2015), and *Gallipoli: The Turkish Defence* (2015). In an April 23, 2009 article titled "Gallipoli: One Great Deception?" Broadbent hypothesized that the Gallipoli Campaign was never meant to succeed, and may have been "conceived and conducted as a ruse to keep the Russians in the war..."[50]

Broadbent speculates that the purpose of the campaign may have been to provide an illusion that the Allies were speeding to Russia's rescue, when, in fact, they were not. The sheer scale and persistence of the alleged "bungling" are difficult to explain by incompetence alone, Broadbent argues, raising the question of deliberate self-sabotage. He writes:

> "It... occurred to me that the under-resourcing, informing the enemy five months in advance of the intention to attack, the hurried and inadequate planning, the overly complicated landing plan on exposed and difficult beaches with no initial massive bombardments to pulverise enemy defences, selection of the most incompetent and timid commanders for a difficult operation and apparent constant bungling that characterised the Allied conduct of the campaign may be attributed to something more than ineptitude.

... Professor Robin Prior, in his new book, *Gallipoli: End of a Myth*, lists a series of decisions and events that he describes as puzzling or incomprehensible."

A QUESTION OF MOTIVE

Let us assume, then, for the sake of argument, that Broadbent is right. Suppose the Allies deliberately sent nearly 57,000 men to their deaths, with no hope of victory. What was their motive?

Broadbent points out that, had the Allies succeeded in taking Constantinople and the Straits, they would have been obliged to turn over these prizes to Russia, in accordance with a secret treaty of March 1915. The Allies would have done all the work, and the Russians reaped the rewards. "Russia alone, will, if the war is successful, gather the fruits of these operations," said a March 15, 1915 memorandum of the British Asquith government, quoted by Broadbent.

In short, honoring the treaty would have done nothing for England. On the contrary, it would have harmed British interests by upending "nearly 200 years of British foreign policy which had opposed a Russian presence in the Mediterranean..." Broadbent notes.

Rather than give the Straits to Russia, the British would have preferred to leave them in the hands of a "shrunken and compliant Ottoman state," Broadbent opines. Such considerations might have led British commanders to conclude that it was better for the attack to fail. "In war thousands of lives are sacrificed for such grand strategies," Broadbent notes.

SAVED BY THE REVOLUTION

Plainly, the British would have preferred not to hand over Constantinople to the Russians. But how could they get out of it? Sabotaging the Gallipoli

Campaign, in and of itself, would not have achieved this goal. The secret treaty—known as the Constantinople Agreement—was inescapable. As long as the Allies won the war, Russia would get her prize. The promise was binding, no matter who won at Gallipoli.

Yet the British got off the hook anyway. What saved them was the Russian Revolution, says Broadbent. "[T]he agreement never had to be honoured ....," he writes. "[T]he Bolshevik Government withdrew from the war and all Tzarist agreements including the Gallipoli treaty."

In short, the Bolsheviks saved the day, by unilaterally withdrawing their claim to Constantinople. This was a great stroke of luck for the British. But was it luck? Or was it planning? Broadbent suggests the latter.

CHAPTER 8

DOUBLE-CROSSING THE TSAR

I F THE RUSSIAN claim to Constantinople was completely unaffected by who won at Gallipoli, then why would the British go to all the trouble of staging a phony attack and making sure they lost (as Broadbent hypothesizes)? Why not go for the win?

In answer, Broadbent poses a hypothetical question. He asks, "If there had been a victory at Gallipoli would there have been a Russian Revolution?" Probably not, says Broadbent. In his opinion, the capture of Constantinople, and its subsequent occupation by Russia, would have caused such an explosion of religious and patriotic fervor in Russia, as to make revolution impossible. Referring to Catherine the Great's plan for a New Byzantium, Broadbent writes:

"With the ultimate re-establishment of a new Byzantine Empire under the Tzar on the new Christian throne in 'Tzaragrad' on the Bosphorus, would the millions of Russian religious peasants, massively influenced by the victory, have flocked to support the Holy Tzar in the face of revolution, thus thwarting the Bolsheviks?"

Broadbent thinks they might have. In that case, the Tsar might have remained on his throne. Such an outcome would have been contrary to British interests, Broadbent suggests.

DID GALLIPOLI CAUSE THE RUSSIAN REVOLUTION?

From the British standpoint, a Russian victory in World War I would have been catastrophic, Broadbent insists. It would have meant that the British and Commonwealth troops at Gallipoli were "fighting not for a war to make the world safe for democracy but for the domination of the Slav world by Tzarist Russia." Broadbent concludes, "*The way out of all this of course was to ensure that Istanbul remained unconquered* [emphasis added]." Lord Kitchener and other high officials of Asquith's government would have been thinking along the same lines, as they made plans for Gallipoli, Broadbent suggests.

Broadbent's arguments are weighty. He compels us to consider whether Britain may have deliberately pulled her punches at Gallipoli precisely in order to deprive the Tsar of the one victory that might have saved his throne.

BARGAINING CHIP

Broadbent's article fails to provide an adequate answer for one important question, however. If the March 1915 agreement was so inimical to British interests, why did Britain make such a treaty in the first place? Why did they offer Constantinople to Russia, if they didn't want Russia to have it?

Broadbent argues that it was bait to keep Russia in the war. No doubt, this is partly true. But there was another reason as well. The British did not offer Constantinople to the Russians for free. They asked something in return. Specifically, they demanded a large chunk of the newly-discovered Persian oil fields. The Russians agreed.[51]

In 1907, Russia and Britain had signed a treaty dividing Persia into two spheres of influence, with the Russians in the north, the British in the south, and a large neutral zone in between. Now, on the eve of the Gallipoli Campaign, the British suddenly asked that the neutral zone be added to the British sphere of influence, greatly enlarging Britain's share of Persia's oil-rich territory. Whatever else we may conclude about the Gallipoli Campaign, it appears to have been a bargaining chip in a high-stakes negotiation over Persian oil.

The three-way Constantinople Agreement was hammered out in a long series of diplomatic letters between France, Britain and Russia from March 4 to April 10, 1915. Opinions vary as to when the Agreement actually became operative. The *Encyclopedia Britannica* gives the date of March 18, 1915, which happens to be the very day the Allied fleet commenced its attack on the Dardanelles. If true, this would suggest that the British held off their attack until the very moment the agreement was settled. The Persian oil concession may very well have been the price the British demanded for attacking Constantinople.

CHAPTER 9

BRITAIN'S WAR PRIZE

I N THE END, the British got much more than the Persian neutral zone. The entire nation of Persia was effectively turned over to Britain, thanks to the unexpected generosity of Leon Trotsky, whose curious connections with British intelligence we have already noted.[52]

Following the Bolshevik coup of November 7, 1917, many perceived Lenin and Trotsky as equals, their regime a two-man junta. "[T]he Lenin-Trotsky combination is all-powerful," the *Times* of London reported on November 19, 1917.[53] However, the day after the coup—on November 8—Trotsky accepted the position of Commissar for Foreign Affairs. This seemingly put him in a subordinate position to Lenin, but it also gave Trotsky tremendous power to alter the course of the war. Perhaps that was the point.

On November 22—two weeks after assuming his new post—Trotsky did a curious thing. He suddenly announced that the Bolshevik government would repudiate all secret treaties and agreements made by previous Russian governments. Trotsky said the treaties had "lost all their obligatory force for the Russian workmen, soldiers, and peasants, who have taken the government into their own hands..."[54] "We sweep all secret treaties into the dustbin," he said.[55] By publishing and repudiating the treaties, Trotsky claimed he was rejecting "Tsarist imperialism."[56] What he was actually doing was enriching the greatest imperial power on earth, Great Britain.

British Petroleum and the Bolsheviks

Among the treaties Trotsky repudiated was the secret Constantinople Agreement of March 18, 1915. He released the British unilaterally from their promise to hand over Constantinople and the Straits.[57] Trotsky likewise repudiated Russia's extensive interests in Persia, including its oil rights, leaving everything for the British.[58]

In August, 1919, the British government took advantage of the Russian withdrawal by claiming all drilling rights in Persia. A British-owned firm called the Anglo-Persian Oil Company (APOC) thus acquired a de facto monopoly over Persian oil. This was a great windfall for the stockholders, especially the British government, which owned a controlling share.

Less than two months before the start of World War I, Asquith's government had taken the unusual step of nationalizing APOC, purchasing a 51-percent share on June 17, 1914.[59] The British government thus positioned itself, shrewdly and presciently, three years in advance, to take direct control of the staggering oil wealth which Trotsky now bestowed upon it.

It may be worth noting that the Persian government never actually agreed to turn over drilling rights to APOC. However, their opinion no longer mattered in 1919.[60] "Russian influence in Persia was reduced to nil and the British... made themselves masters in all of Persia," wrote US journalist Louis Fischer in his 1926 book *Oil Imperialism*.[61]

Trotsky's revolutionary rhetoric notwithstanding, these actions brought no benefit to the Russian people. They helped only the British.

The Anglo-Persian Oil Company was now free to expand, since its chief rival, the Russian Empire, had suddenly vanished into thin air. In 1935, the fast-growing British oil giant changed its name to the Anglo-Iranian Oil Company, then to British Petroleum in 1954.

BACKLASH

If Harvey Broadbent is correct—if the British really did pull their punches at Gallipoli to prevent Russia from winning the war—then it appears their ruse was successful. The collapse of Russia brought the Bolsheviks to power, allowing Trotsky to hand over to Britain the greatest oil deposits known to exist at that time. Never before had Britain acquired so much wealth, so quickly. Never before had she wielded such disproportionate power in the world (given her size), not even at the height of Queen Victoria's reign.

But the British had overplayed their hand. Their greed had made them reckless. Britain's seizure of the Persian oil fields aroused envy and indignation even from her allies. Moreover, the crimes of the Bolsheviks were coming to light, horrifying the world. Credible witnesses such as Princess Paley were accusing Great Britain of toppling the Tsar and backing the Bolsheviks.

The mood in the streets was dangerous. People were asking questions. Secrets were coming out. It was only a matter of time before even deeper secrets were laid bare, including one particular secret Britain could not afford to disclose. This, I believe, was the specter haunting Churchill when he penned his anti-Jewish screed in 1920.

With all the outrage, inquisitiveness, and increased scrutiny following World War I, Churchill feared that Britain's ultimate secret—the jewel in the crown of her clandestine services—might be revealed. The true source of British power would then be exposed, a weapon so shrouded in mystery that few suspected its existence. Deployed many times, in many countries, over the last 150 years, this weapon had made Great Britain master of the earth. British leaders could not afford to let it out. They would do anything to keep it under wraps.

PART III

HOW THE BRITISH INVENTED
COLOR REVOLUTIONS

CHAPTER 10

BRITAIN'S SECRET WEAPON

GREAT BRITAIN HAD a weapon no one else had. They could make their enemies vanish into thin air. Upon a signal, governments would fall. Markets would crash. Armies would mutiny. Rioters would take to the streets. Such was the skill of Britain's clandestine services, that they often won wars without firing a shot, and often with no one even suspecting that a war had been fought.

Nowadays, we call such invisible wars "color revolutions." The term became popular in the West after the break-up of the USSR, when numerous post-Soviet states experienced what appeared to be waves of popular revolts, one after another. These were not ordinary uprisings. They seemed to have an eerie, almost magical, power to topple governments without violence. Crowds of young people would march through the streets, decked out in identifying "team colors" or symbols, such as orange for Ukraine's 2004 Orange Revolution or roses for post-Soviet Georgia's 2003 Rose Revolution. And somehow this worked. To the astonishment of the world, armies stood down, police looked the other way, national leaders fled the country, and governments fell. It was all very strange.

WEAPONS OF WAR

The so-called "color revolutions" were portrayed in Western media as spontaneous uprisings. But they were far from spontaneous, as David Horowitz and I revealed in our 2006 book *The Shadow Party*. We exposed the role of George Soros and his Open Society Foundations in helping to fund and orchestrate many of these insurgencies.[62] We noted that Soros worked hand-in-hand with a global network of government-aligned front groups.[63] Most importantly, we ascertained that color revolutions succeed not through the magical power of flowers and colored ribbons, but rather through years of preparatory work carried out covertly by trained operators.

In *The Shadow Party*, we noted that post-Soviet color revolutions all seemed to follow a playbook written by the late Gene Sharp, an American political scientist who is often described, misleadingly, as a peace activist.[64] In fact, Sharp was a psywar operative, with strong ties to both US and British intelligence.

"STRATEGIC NON-VIOLENCE" INVENTED AT OXFORD

Sharp spent 30 years at the Center for International Affairs, nicknamed the "CIA at Harvard."[65] More importantly, he spent 10 years in England (1955 to 1965), working with the British peace movement and earning a Ph.D. from Oxford. Sharp's iconic work, his 1973 book *The Politics of Nonviolent Action* happens to have been Sharp's Oxford doctoral thesis.

It is widely regarded as the original "playbook" for color revolution.

Sharp's mentors in England included some of the top names in British military intelligence, including Basil Liddell Hart and Stephen King-Hall, both pioneers in the development of "strategic non-violence" as a weapon of war.[66] It was they who taught Sharp to topple governments under the guise of "people's revolutions." The British have been cultivating this dark art for centuries.

INFILTRATION AND SUBVERSION

Sharp's British mentors taught him that spontaneous uprisings cannot overthrow governments. The brute force of the state can easily suppress such disorders. Revolutions succeed only when the security forces themselves stand down and let it happen, as they did in France and Russia in 1789 and 1917 respectively. But why would the security forces stand down? Only one thing can cause this. Leaders in key positions must be compromised. David Horowitz and I wrote in *The Shadow Party*:

> "The key to defeating a hostile government, Sharp taught, was to undermine the ability to fight its opponents. This was a slow process, requiring patient infiltration of strategic departments of the target government, especially the police, military and intelligence communities."[67]

Obviously, infiltrating the "police, military and intelligence communities" is not a job for amateurs. It requires trained intelligence professionals, with state support. But that part is secret, kept hidden from the media. It is precisely in the staging of such deceptions that British spymasters have excelled. Their centuries-old methods for disguising coups as people's revolutions constitute what I call Britain's "ultimate secret," the weapon whose existence Churchill needed to hide in 1920.

WHAT IS A COLOR REVOLUTION?

If we define a color revolution as a fake insurrection—that is, as a foreign-sponsored coup masquerading as a people's uprising—then we must conclude that the French Revolution of 1789 and the Russian Revolution of 1917 seem to fit that description.

In both cases, the uprisings began not in the streets, but in the drawing rooms of liberal aristocrats. In both cases, the hidden hand of British intelligence can be found manipulating events behind the scenes. In both cases, "team colors" were used to identify the rebels, in a manner similar to today's color revolutions—specifically, the tricolor cockade and "Phrygian" cap of the French Revolution, and the red flag and "Scythian" cap of the Bolsheviks.

A 150-YEAR COVER STORY

As noted in Chapter 9, the British government plainly had much to hide in its relationship with the Bolsheviks. It therefore sought to deflect blame onto others, such as the Jews. However, Churchill's 1920 article in the *Illustrated Sunday Herald* went further. Churchill did not just blame the Jews for the Bolshevik Revolution. He blamed them for literally "every subversive movement during the 19th century." Churchill alleged a 150-year conspiracy, dating back to the Bavarian Illuminati of Adam Weishaupt and the French Revolution of 1789. He wrote:

> "This movement among the Jews is not new. From the days of Spartacus-Weishaupt to those of Karl Marx, and down to Trotsky ... this worldwide conspiracy for the overthrow of civilisation... has been steadily growing. It played... a definitely recognisable part in the tragedy of the French Revolution. It has been the mainspring of every subversive movement during the 19th century..."[68]

What did Churchill mean by this? Was he simply exaggerating for dramatic effect? Indulging in a bit of rhetorical overkill? Or was his reference to a 150-year conspiracy purposeful and calculated? I would say it was calculated. Churchill's allegation of a centuries-old conspiracy appears to be yet another cover story, calculated to distract from yet another sensitive subject which the British government had reason to hide.

CHURCHILL'S SECRET

When Churchill accused the Jews of fomenting "every subversive movement" since the Illuminati and the French Revolution, I believe he was trying to deflect attention from the fact that the British government itself had been the primary funder and instigator of revolutionary movements since the 18th century. The mechanisms Britain had created for funding, inciting, and executing such revolutions constituted a potent weapons system whose very existence was a state secret and without which there would have been no British Empire.

It is no coincidence that the so-called Age of Revolution coincided with Britain's rise to global dominance. It was precisely during that era— the late 18th to early 20th centuries—that Britain mastered the use of political subversion as a weapon of statecraft, an instrument for toppling governments that stood in her way.

Blaming Jews for this long history of "color revolutions" proved an efficient way to distract attention from British involvement. Still, from the very beginning, there were a few attentive observers who saw through the smokescreen and recognized the hand of Great Britain behind these revolutionary movements. One was Thomas Jefferson, whose eyewitness account of the French Revolution leaves little doubt of British complicity.

CHAPTER 11

HOW THE BRITISH CAUSED THE FRENCH REVOLUTION

KING LOUIS XVI was Britain's number one enemy when the French Revolution broke out. He had earned Britain's hatred by intervening in the American Revolution, forcing Britain to grant independence to the Thirteen Colonies. The British never forgave him. They devised a plan for Louis's removal.

They did not have to wait long for their revenge. The growing demand for liberal reform in France provided an opening. Inspired by America's revolution, many in France hoped for a better world, in which rank and privilege would give way to liberty and equality.

French liberals of that time tended to be Anglophilic. They looked to England as a beacon of liberty—as much as America—seeing both countries as products of a common tradition of English freedom.[69] The British secret services took advantage of this good will. Intelligence operatives posing as English reformers infiltrated the French intelligentsia, pushing French dissidents toward violence, class warfare, and hatred of the Bourbon dynasty.

THE REVOLUTION HIJACKED

No less an authority than Thomas Jefferson accused the British of using "hired" agents of influence to subvert the French Revolution. Jefferson was in a position to know, as he had been US ambassador to France when the Revolution broke out in 1789. Jefferson and the Marquis de Lafayette had hoped the uprising would bring constitutional monarchy to France, leaving Louis XVI safely on his throne. But this was not to be.

In a letter of February 14, 1815, Jefferson wrote Lafayette, lamenting the failure of the French Revolution, and blaming it on British intrigue.[70] The British had subverted the Revolution, Jefferson wrote, by sending "hired pretenders" to "crush in their own councils the genuine republicans," thus turning the Revolution toward "destruction" and the "unprincipled and bloody tyranny of Robespierre..." By such means, wrote Jefferson, "the foreigner" overthrew "by gold the government he could not overthrow by arms"—as apt a description of a color revolution as one could imagine.

PAID AGENTS

Jefferson expressed the same view in a letter of January 31, 1815 to William Plumer, a New Hampshire lawyer and politician.[71] "[W]hen England took alarm lest France, become republican, should recover energies dangerous to her," wrote Jefferson, "she employed emissaries with means to engage incendiaries and anarchists in the disorganisation of all government there..."

According to Jefferson, these hired "incendiaries and anarchists" infiltrated the Revolution by "assuming exaggerated zeal for republican government," then gained control of the legislature, "overwhelming by their majorities the honest & enlightened patriots..." These paid agents "intrigued themselves into the municipality of Paris," said Jefferson, "controlled by terrorism the proceedings of the legislature…" and finally "murdered the king," thus "demolishing liberty and government with it." In the same letter, Jefferson accused Danton and Marat by name of being on the British payroll.

THE LONDON REVOLUTION SOCIETY

Jefferson's views find unexpected support from US historian Micah Alpaugh, who has revealed the extensive influence British reformers exerted over the French revolutionaries. Unlike Jefferson, Alpaugh sees nothing nefarious in this influence, but nonetheless remarks on its surprising extent.

In his 2014 paper, "The British Origins of the French Jacobins," Alpaugh notes that France's radical Jacobin clubs were consciously modeled after an existing British organization, the London Revolution Society (sometimes called the London Revolutionary Society).[72] This was a group of English intellectuals who began meeting at the London Tavern in Bishopsgate in 1788, ostensibly to celebrate the 100-year anniversary of William III's Glorious Revolution. It soon became clear, however, that their true goal was to agitate for revolution in the present day.

BRITISH RADICALS INTERVENE

On November 25, 1789—four months after the storming of the Bastille—King Louis XVI was still on his throne, showing every willingness to work with the new National Assembly to form a constitutional monarchy. But this was not to be. Forces were hard at work in the shadows determined to unseat King Louis from his throne.

That day, November 25, 1789, the president of the French National

Assembly read aloud to the legislators a letter from the London radicals. The letter directly inspired the formation of the so-called Jacobin clubs, from which Danton, Marat, Robespierre, and the Reign of Terror would later emerge. The letter seemed innocent enough on the surface, calling on the French to disdain "National partialities" and join with their English brethren in a revolution that would make "the World free and happy." But deceptive agendas lay hidden between the lines.

A "GROWING ANGLOPHILIA"

Alpaugh writes that the letter "produced a 'great sensation' and loud applause in the hall. The French Assembly wrote back to London declaring how it had seen 'the aurora of the beautiful day' when the two nations could put aside their differences and 'contract an intimate liaison by the similarity of their opinions, and by their common enthusiasm for liberty'."

This letter fueled what Alpaugh calls a "growing Anglophilia," inspiring the French revolutionaries to found a Societé de la Révolution, directly modeled after the London Revolutionary Society. The Societé de la Révolution was later renamed, but always kept its English-style nickname *Club des Jacobins*—pointedly retaining the English word "club" as a tribute to the group's British origin, Alpaugh explains.[73]

THE POISONED CHALICE

As Jacobin "clubs" sprang up all over France, they typically retained close ties to their English mentors. Alpaugh writes, "Early French Jacobins created their network in consultation with British models," such as the London Revolution Society and the London Corresponding Society. "Direct correspondence between British and French radical organizations between 1787 and 1793 would develop reciprocal and mutually inspiring relationships…helping inspire the rise of Jacobin Clubs through-out France," writes Alpaugh.[74]

Deliberately or not, the so-called "English Jacobins" (as they came to be known) offered their French disciples a poisoned chalice of "cosmo-politanism, internationalism, and universalism" (Alpaugh's words), urging the French idealists to put aside the narrow interests of their own country, in favor of the broader interests of mankind.[75]

This was, in fact, a deception. Alpaugh may not see it this way, but the broader interests of mankind pushed by the "English Jacobins" turned out to be little more than a smokescreen for British imperial interests. The Jacobin Clubs gave rise to Marat, Danton, and Robespierre, ultimately leading to the Reign of Terror and the murder of King Louis XVI. They also gave rise to a new ideology which has come to be known as communism.

CHAPTER 12

THE INVENTION OF COMMUNISM

OMMUNISM WAS BORN on the streets of revolutionary Paris. More than fifty years before Marx and Engels penned *The Communist Manifesto*, a faction of French radicals calling itself the Conspiracy of Equals was already preaching classless society, abolition of private property, and the need for revolutionary action.

Led by "Gracchus" Babeuf—whose real name was François-Noël Babeuf—the Conspiracy of Equals tried unsuccessfully to overthrow the so-called Directory, France's last revolutionary government, in 1796.[76] Their conspiracy failed, and Babeuf was put to death. But his ideas live on. Marx and Engels called Babeuf the first modern communist.[77]

No record exists of Babeuf using the word *communiste*, though he sometimes called his followers "*communautistes*" (usually translated "communitarian").[78] However, a contemporary of Babeuf, Nicolas Restif de la Bretonne, often used the word "communist" in his writings, beginning as early as 1785.[79] Babeuf's prosecutors apparently believed that Restif was secretly in league with the Conspiracy of

Equals, and some evidence suggests they may have been, according to James Billington, in his 1980 book *Fire in the Minds of Men: Origins of the Revolutionary Faith*.[80]

JACOBIN COMMUNISM

For all these reasons, it is not surprising that the self-styled *"communistes"* who emerged in Paris during the 1830s and 1840s saw themselves, at least partly, as following in the footsteps of Babeuf.[81] Marxist historian David Fernbach wrote in 1973:

> "The term 'communism' in the France of the 1840s denoted… an offshoot of the Jacobin tradition of the first French revolution. (…) This communism went back to Gracchus Babeuf's Conspiracy of Equals… This egalitarian or 'crude' communism, as Marx called it originated before the great development of machine industry. It appealed to the Paris *sans-culottes*—artisans, journeymen and unemployed—and potentially to the poor peasantry in the countryside."[82]

Thus, Babeuf's "crude" communism was already shaking up Paris more than 20 years before Marx was born. By March, 1840, the Communist movement in Paris was deemed sufficiently threatening that a German newspaper denounced it, saying, "The Communists have in view nothing less than a levelling of society—substituting for the presently-existing order of things the absurd, immoral and impossible utopia of a community of goods."[83] When these words were written, the 21-year-old Karl Marx was studying classics and philosophy in Berlin. He had not yet shown a strong interest in radical or revolutionary politics.

BABEUF'S BRITISH MENTORS

Babeuf's status as the founding father of communism cannot be disputed. It is therefore significant that Babeuf derived many of his ideas from British mentors, at least some of whom were British intelligence operatives. In that respect, Babeuf followed a path trod by many other French revolutionaries.

One of Babeuf's mentors was James Rutledge, an Englishman living in Paris, who called himself a "citizen of the universe" and preached the abolition of private ownership.[84] "Babeuf had known Rutledge even before the revolution," writes Billington in *Fire in the Minds of Men* (1980). Through Rutledge and his circle, Babeuf became acquainted with the *Courrier de l'Europe*, a French-language newspaper published in London and distributed in France. It promoted such radical doctrines as the overthrow of the French aristocracy and the establishment of a classless society. Babeuf became a regular correspondent of the paper in 1789.[85]

It appears to have been a British intelligence front. The newspaper's owner was London wine merchant Samuel Swinton, a former lieutenant in the Royal Navy who had, in the past, performed sensitive diplomatic missions for Prime Minister Lord North. In a 1985 paper, French historian Hélène Maspero Clerc concluded that Swinton was a British secret agent, based upon her study of Swinton's correspondence with British Secretary of the Admiralty Philip Stephens.[86]

Thus the hidden hand of British intelligence can be found guiding and helping Babeuf—the first modern communist—from early in his career. The same can be said of another early communist, Karl Marx.

Part IV

How Marxism Serves the Empire

CHAPTER 13

KARL MARX, BRITISH AGENT

KARL MARX'S CAREER followed a trajectory similar to that of the French revolutionaries. Like them, Marx was influenced by British mentors, at least some of whom are known to have been intelligence operatives. In Marx's case, the British influence was arguably stronger than it had been with Babeuf. For one thing, Marx had family connections to the British aristocracy. In 1843, he married Jenny von Westphalen. Her father was a Prussian baron, whose Scottish mother, Jeanie Wishart, descended from the Earls of Argyll.[87]

In 1847, Marx and Engels were commissioned by the London-based Communist League to write the *Communist Manifesto*. The tract was published first in London, in 1848.[88] Expelled from Prussia, France, and Belgium for his subversive activities, Marx and his family took refuge in England in 1849. He lived in London for the rest of his life.

IMPERIAL PROPAGANDIST

History is filled with men like Marx who supposedly pulled themselves up by their bootstraps, succeeding through ability alone. Yet, closer inspection often reveals that such "self-made" men relied upon influential relatives to open doors for them. Karl Marx was such a man.

In February, 1854, Marx met Scottish nobleman David Urquhart (pronounced ERK-art)—apparently a distant relative of Marx's wife, through her Scottish grandmother.[89] Urquhart was a British diplomat and sometime secret agent, who became a kind of 19th-century version of Lawrence of Arabia. After fighting in the Greek War of Independence, Urquhart served as a diplomat in Constantinople, where he became a close confidant of the Sultan. In 1834, Urquhart instigated a rebellion against Russia among the Circassian tribes of the Caucasus. The Circassians named him Daud Bey (Chief David). The name stuck, becoming famous throughout the Middle East.[90]

Urquhart had a fanatical hatred of Russia, so intense that he publicly accused Lord Palmerston, the Prime Minister, of being a paid Russian agent.[91] Somewhat surprisingly, Marx joined Urquhart's cause, becoming one of the most prominent anti-Russian journalists of his day. Marx wrote blistering anti-Russian screeds for *The New York Tribune*—then the highest-circulation newspaper in the world—as well as for Urquhart's own publications in Britain.[92]

Marx went so far as to echo Urquhart's accusation that Lord Palmerston was secretly in league with the Russians.[93] In his attacks on Russia, Marx wrote not as a revolutionary, but as a propagandist for British imperial interests. His tirades against Russia proved useful to the Empire during the Crimean War of 1853-1856.

CHAPTER 14

MARX'S ARISTOCRATIC HANDLER

THE ALLIANCE BETWEEN Marx and Urquhart has confounded historians for generations. Marx was a communist and Urquhart an arch-reactionary. What bound them together? What could they possibly have had in common? Many scholars have simply ignored this question. Some have actively tried to suppress it, by concealing the very existence of Marx's anti-Russian work. In his 1999 biography *Karl Marx: A Life*, Francis Wheen writes:

"His [Marx's] philippics against Palmerston and Russia were reissued in 1899 by his daughter Eleanor as two pamphlets, *The Secret Diplomatic History of the Eighteenth Century* and *The Story of the Life of Lord Palmerston*—though with some of the more provocative passages quietly excised. For most of the twentieth century they remained out of print and largely forgotten. The Institute of Marxism-Leninism in Moscow omitted them from its otherwise exhaustive *Collected Works*, presumably because the Soviet editors could not bring themselves to admit that the presiding spirit of the Russian revolution had in fact been a fervent Russophobe. Marxist hagiographers in the West have also been reluctant to draw attention to this embarrassing partnership between the revolutionist and the reactionary. An all-too-typical example is *The Life and Teaching of Karl Marx* by John Lewis, published in 1965; the curious reader may search the text for any mention of David Urquhart, or of Marx's contribution to his obsessive crusade but will find nothing."[94]

"KINDRED SOULS"

In his 1910 biography, *Karl Marx: His Life and Work*, John Spargo argues that, "Marx gladly cooperated with David Urquhart and his followers in their anti-Russian campaign, for he regarded Russia as the leading reactionary Power in the world, and never lost an opportunity of expressing his hatred of it."[95] Spargo thus tries to explain Marx's anti-Russian work in terms of an ideological aversion to Russia's "reactionary" politics, which is to say, Russia's feudal condition during the 1850s, whereby the Tsar held absolute power, and the landowning nobility kept more than 20 million peasants in a state of serfdom.

This interpretation does not pass muster, however. In all of Britain, there was no more "reactionary" voice than David Urquhart, who openly called for a restoration of the feudal system. In his 1845 book *Wealth and Want*, Urquhart argued that a serf under feudalism was better off than the paupers, miners, and factory workers of the present industrial age.[96] "Serfdom, I assert, to have been a better condition than dependent labour..." Urquhart wrote. "The villain was not the slave of the lord, but... a freer man than any labourer to-day." If Marx hated reaction, why then was he drawn to David Urquhart, whose "reactionary" views surely rivaled those of the most retrograde Russian landlord?

John Spargo writes: "In David Urquhart he [Marx] found a kindred soul to whom he became greatly attached. ...The influence which David Urquhart obtained over Marx was remarkable. Marx probably never relied upon the judgment of another man as he did upon that of Urquhart."[97] The alliance between Marx and Urquhart confronts us with a genuine mystery. If it is true that Marx found a "kindred soul" in Urquhart, then their views must have converged, in ways beyond the obvious. What exactly did these men have in common?

CHAPTER 15

WAR AGAINST THE
MIDDLE CLASS

I BELIEVE WHAT BONDED Marx and Urquhart was their mutual hatred of the
middle class. This was the era of Young England, a movement of landed
aristocrats calling for a return to the feudal system.[98] While Urquhart is not
normally mentioned in connection with the parliamentary faction calling itself Young England, he certainly shared its views. The Industrial Revolution
had turned British society upside down, forcing men, women, and children
of the lower classes to toil long hours in mines and factories under appalling
conditions and for meager pay. The aristocrats of Young England blamed these
abuses on the vulgar, money-grubbing culture of the middle class or *bourgeoisie*.

Things had been better in the Middle Ages, the Young Englanders argued. In those days, benevolent landlords cared for their serfs, as lovingly
as they cared for their hounds and horses, never letting them go hungry
or homeless. The problem of "pauperism" would vanish, said the Young
Englanders, if the landowning gentry were put back in charge. The aristocrat's ancient sense of *noblesse oblige* would motivate blue-bloods to provide for the poor, just as they always had in the past.

"EXTINGUISH THE PREDOMINANCE OF THE MIDDLE-CLASS BOURGEOISIE"

To prove their point, the aristocrats of Young England became reformers in the 1840s, agitating for a ten-hour work day and other policies to help the poor and working class. To achieve these ends, the Young Englanders allied themselves with communists and socialists, who hated the "bourgeoisie" as much as they did, albeit for different reasons.[99]

The Young England movement, "sought to *extinguish the predominance of the middle-class bourgeoisie* [emphasis added], and to recreate the political prestige of the aristocracy by resolutely proving its capacity to ameliorate the social, intellectual, and material condition of the peasantry and the labouring classes," states the 1902 *Encyclopedia Britannica*.[100] The key phrase here is "*extinguish the predominance of the middle-class bourgeoisie*"—a goal the Young Englanders shared with their communist and socialist allies.

Thus the Young England movement brought Tory aristocrats such as Lord John Manners and George Smythe into alliance with socialist firebrands such as Robert Owen and Joseph Rayner Stephens.[101] Ultimately, it would bring David Urquhart into alliance with Karl Marx.

"NATURAL ALLIANCE"

The Anglo-Irish writer Kenelm Henry Digby has been widely acknowledged as the spiritual leader of Young England. His trilogy *The Broad Stone of Honour*—written between 1829 and 1848—served as the movement's "handbook" or "breviary" (prayerbook), according to Charles Whibley's 1925 history of the movement, *Lord John Manners and His Friends*.[102] Whibley writes: "And he [Digby] found in the champions of Young England his most willing pupils, because... he admitted that the aristocracy and the people formed a natural alliance..."

Regarding this "natural alliance" between nobility and peasantry, Whibley quotes Digby as follows: "I pronounce that there is ever a peculiar connection, a sympathy of feeling and affection, a kind of fellowship which is instantly felt and recognised by both, between these [the lower classes] and the highest order, that of gentlemen. In society, as in the atmosphere of the world, *it is the middle which is the region of disorder and confusion and tempest* [emphasis added]."[103] By "the middle," Digby plainly means the "middle class."

Like Marx, Digby saw the bourgeoisie as a disturbing new force in the world, breaking the old "natural alliance" between lord and serf, and sowing "disorder," "confusion" and "tempest." Marx may or may not have read Digby, but his view of the middle class is undeniably Digby-esque.

CHAPTER 16

MYTH OF THE BOURGEOIS REVOLUTION

"I T IS NOT the abolition of property generally which distinguishes Communism; It is the abolition of Bourgeois property," wrote Marx in *The Communist Manifesto* (1848). [104] By distinguishing between "bourgeois property" and "property generally" Marx meant that his new Communist movement would not focus on fighting the landowning gentry because— according to Marx—that battle had already been won. The real power in today's world, Marx insisted, was no longer the feudal lord, but the bourgeois businessman, who had supposedly overthrown the aristocrats in a series of bourgeois revolutions.

Today, it is universally accepted that the old aristocracy is extinct. Whatever remnants of it may linger, hiding away in musty drawing rooms of places like Buckingham Palace, they are deemed to be powerless, unimportant, and financially insignificant. In their place, we are now asked to believe, self-made entrepreneurs such as Bill Gates and Elon Musk have become the richest, most powerful men on earth.

In reality, we have no way of knowing who the wealthiest people are, as wealth is routinely hidden in offshore trusts, beneath layers of shell corporations, where it cannot be traced. There are, in fact, indications that—contrary to Marx's theory of bourgeois revolution—certain aristocratic families not only managed to survive the Industrial Revolution with their wealth and power intact, but learned to thrive in the new system, living quietly, out of sight, and letting the bourgeoisie get all the limelight.

THE PERSISTENT POWER OF THE ARISTOCRACY

More than 70 years after Marx and Engels pronounced the feudal aristocracy dead, the power of Britain's landed nobility emerged unexpectedly as a topic of heated debate in the US Senate. In 1919, the Senate was pondering the question of whether or not to ratify the Versailles Treaty, which would have required the US to join the League of Nations. Public opinion ran strongly against ratification, as most Americans—not unreasonably—feared the League of Nations would draw the US back into a dependent relationship with the British Empire.

Daniel F. Cohalan, a justice of the New York Supreme Court, appeared before the Senate Foreign Affairs Committee on August 30, 1919, to argue against ratification. Born in New York, of Irish descent, Cohalan was active in the Irish Republican movement. He claimed to speak for America's 20 million citizens of Irish descent, which is to say, for one in five Americans alive at that time.[105] "We believe we went to war for the purpose of ending autocracy…," Cohalan told the Foreign Affairs Committee.[106] Yet the British Empire represented, "the most absolute, most arbitrary and most powerful autocracy the world has ever seen," he declared.[107]

"[T]HE REAL RULING FORCE IS... THE LANDED FEUDAL ARISTOCRACY OF ENGLAND..."

Cohalan's testimony on this point is worth quoting at length. He told the US Senate:

> "The ordinary American… has not come to understand that the English democracy of which he hears and reads so much has little reality in fact, and that England continues to be governed by a handful of men, representing, with but few exceptions, the same small group of titled land-controlling families that have governed England since the days of Henry VIII, if not, in fact, much longer. …

> "*The dominating figures in England to-day—those in actual power— are the Cecils and their relations.* [emphasis added]. Lloyd-George or some other figure that has come to represent democracy… is put forward as the premier of governing authority. But the will that dominates, controls, and finally directs the policies and actions of England is that of the master spirit Cecil, no matter which member of that family or its connections it may happen to be. …

> "Englishmen like to say that King George reigns but does not rule. That is true. The real ruling force is that handful of aristocrats who represent the landed feudal aristocracy of England and who form the most absolute, most arbitrary and most powerful autocracy the world has ever seen."[108]

This is not the place to debate the question of who really runs things in this world, but Judge Cohalan's testimony at least reminds us that the obvious and familiar answers are not necessarily the right ones.

The "Naked, Shameless, Brutal" Bourgeoisie

Like his aristocratic mentor Urquhart, Marx had a tendency to romanticize the "idyllic" feudal past, and to vilify middle-class culture, in terms reminiscent of the Young Englanders. That is not to say that Marx approved of the feudal order. He clearly opposed it. Nonetheless, Marx plainly saw the bourgeois order as worse.

Marx imagined the Middle Ages as offering, at the very least, some comforting illusion of a harmonious natural order, based on "patriarchal" relations, chivalry, and faith. The money-grubbing bourgeoisie, on the other hand, had stripped away those illusions, leaving only "naked, shameless, direct, brutal exploitation," said Marx. He spelled it out in the *Communist Manifesto*. Marx wrote:

> "The bourgeoisie, wherever it has got the upper hand, has put an end to all feudal, patriarchal, idyllic relations. It has pitilessly torn asunder the motley feudal ties that bound man to his 'natural superiors', and has left remaining no other nexus between man and man than naked self-interest, than callous 'cash payment'. It has drowned the most heavenly ecstasies of religious fervour, of chivalrous enthusiasm, of philistine sentimentalism, in the icy water of egotistical calculation. It has resolved personal worth into exchange value, and in place of the numberless indefeasible chartered freedoms, has set up that single, unconscionable freedom—Free Trade. In one word, for exploitation, veiled by religious and political illusions, it has substituted naked, shameless, direct, brutal exploitation."[109]

Digby himself could not have said it better.

YOUNG ENGLAND LIVES ON

Most historians hold that the Young England movement petered out around 1849. Yet the spirit of Young England lived on, under different guises. It survived through the strange, symbiotic relationship between Urquhart and Marx. It lingered, through the 1880s, in the teachings of Oxford professor John Ruskin, and two of his young disciples, Arnold Toynbee and Alfred Milner.[110]

The Ruskinites embraced a philosophy that would one day come to be known as "liberal imperialism"—the notion that the best way to spread enlightened social policies across the world was by conquest and colonization, that is, through expansion of the British Empire.

Milner would go on to become one of Britain's leading statesmen. He served as colonial governor of southern Africa during the Boer Wars, and as War Secretary for Lloyd George during World War I. In 1920, the deposed premier of Russia, Alexander Kerensky, would call Milner the "wicked genius of Russia," a reference to Milner's controversial role in stirring up the Russian Revolution.[111] But that's getting ahead of our story.

CHAPTER 17

THE MAN WHO BROUGHT DOWN THE TSAR

IN 1882, MILNER was just an idealistic young journalist filled with enthusiasm for imperialism and social reform. In that year—the last year of Marx's life—Toynbee and Milner both gave lecture series on the topic of socialism.[112] Both praised Marx as a genius. Both argued, intriguingly, that socialism was Britain's secret weapon for containing and heading off revolution.

The core of their argument was pure Young Englandism—the idea that the upper classes could save Britain from revolution by giving socialism to the masses. They further claimed—once again in the spirit of Young England—that the middle class, or bourgeoisie, was the biggest obstacle to their goal. These 1882 lectures of Toynbee and Milner were so similar in form and subject matter that I will quote from both below, alternately allowing Toynbee and Milner to complete each other's thoughts.

HEADING OFF REVOLUTION

Milner began by acknowledging Marx's core argument that the Industrial Revolution had intensified class conflict to the point that revolution was imminent. However, England could escape revolution if she acted wisely, said Milner. He said:

> "The industrial revolution in England is the type and forerunner of that which has swept over every country in Europe. We got through it sooner, we experienced its evils sooner, perhaps we shall find hereafter that we have begun to discover the remedies for these evils sooner than any other nation."[113]

And what were those remedies? "Socialist programmes," said Toynbee.[114] Toynbee argued that, of all countries, England was least likely to experience a revolution, because she had had the foresight to implement "socialist programmes" before it was too late.

"Some of the things the Socialists of Germany and France are now working for, we have had since 1834," Toynbee boasted. In this regard, Toynbee cited the New Poor Law of 1834, which had established workhouses for the poor, and the various Factory Acts, such as those of 1847 and 1848, which had established a 10-hour work day as well as other improvements in work conditions. Such measures, said Toynbee, had "saved England from revolution."

THE BOURGEOIS THREAT

Toynbee expressly credited the Young England movement for these enlightened policies, praising Lord John Manners by name. "[L]et us recognize the fact plainly," said Toynbee, "that it is because there has been a ruling aristocracy in England that we have had a great Socialist programme carried out. ... [T]he supremacy of the landowners, which has been the cause of so much injustice and suffering, has also been the means of averting revolution."[115]

Milner and Toynbee both agreed that the best way to head off revolution was by meeting the revolutionaries halfway and giving them some form of socialism. Like the Young Englanders before them, Milner and Toynbee recognized a "natural alliance" between the upper and lower classes. It was the middle class, the bourgeoisie, that posed a problem.

Milner pointed squarely to the middle class as the greatest threat to social stability. He condemned what he called, "the dominant principles of economics, the middle-class or bourgeois principles which have been invented by Capitalists to justify the Capitalistic system and to maintain it."[116]

COMMUNISM: "THE ULTIMATE FORM OF HUMAN SOCIETY"

Milner continued: "The fundamental doctrine of the dominant [middle-class] school—and on reflection I think the Socialists are justified in calling it dominant, it is dominant in Parliament, in the Press, in nine-tenths of our laws and institutions... the doctrine of this dominant bourgeois or middle-class economy is that the whole business of the State is to protect the personal freedom and the property of the individual."[117]

However, Milner saw a new order on the horizon, one in which the "bourgeois or middle-class" values of "personal freedom" and "property" would no longer dominate men's thinking. "I don't deny that Communism may be the ultimate form of human society," Milner stated, though he allowed that "pure Communism" might be "impracticable" for the present age.[118]

Impractical or not, Milner had high praise for Karl Marx. In an 1882 lecture on the "German Socialists," Milner called Marx, "one of the most weighty, logical and learned of reasoners," adding, "Marx's great book *Das Kapital* is at once a monument of reasoning and a storehouse of facts."[119] Strangely and fatefully, the same Alfred Milner who praised Marx in 1882 ended up, thirty-five years later, playing a major role in bringing the first Marxist state into being.

PART V

THE BLOODBATH

CHAPTER 18

LORD MILNER'S COUP

I N FEBRUARY, 1917, Lord Milner traveled to Petrograd to warn the Tsar that Russia was on the brink of revolution. To save the monarchy, the Tsar must lay down his traditional autocratic powers and institute democratic government, Milner told him.[120] Nicholas refused.

In fact, Milner's demand was unreasonable. To democratize Russia in the midst of war would have been folly. Britain had done exactly the opposite, creating a five-man War Cabinet in December, 1916, endowed with extraordinary powers which many called dictatorial. France too had radically streamlined its government decision-making for the war.[121] Germany had turned over its government to what was, in effect, a two-man military junta, consisting of Field Marshall Paul von Hindenberg and General Erich Ludendorff.

If there was a good time for Russia to democratize, February 1917 was not it. Milner was giving Nicholas bad advice on purpose. He was trying to manipulate the Tsar into surrendering power to the Duma, knowing that the Duma's liberal leaders were all in the pockets of the British Embassy.

REVOLUTION FROM ABOVE

Milner left Petrograd on February 27. Nine days later, the Revolution began.[122] On March 8, 1917 a sudden cut in food rations triggered riots in Petrograd.[123] The city garrison mutinied on March 12. The Tsar abdicated on March 15.[124]

This was the so-called February Revolution (given that name because the old Russian calendar ran 13 days late; Russians therefore dated the start of the food riots February 24 instead of March 8). To avoid confusion, all dates here will be in New Style, not Old Style.

The February Revolution had been well-planned. It was a revolution from above, not below. When the soldiers mutinied, they did not rampage through the streets. They marched straight to the Tauride Palace, where the Duma met, to pledge their loyalty to Russia's new rulers.

The London *Daily Telegraph* of March 17, 1917 reported: "On Tuesday [March 12] the movement rapidly spread to all the regiments of the garrison, and one by one they came marching up to the Duma to offer their services. ... [T]hey listened to speeches from MM. Rodzianko, Miliukoff, and Kerenski, and then marched off amid cheering."[125]

Grand Duke Cyril Vladimirovich—first cousin to the Tsar, and third in line to the throne—also marched to the Duma that day, in his naval captain's uniform, leading the Marine Guard whom he commanded.[126] "I wish to declare my sympathy for the new regime, and to place myself at your disposal," the Grand Duke told Duma President Mikhail Rodzianko.[127] It may be worth noting that Grand Duke Cyril had an English wife, Princess Victoria of Edinburgh, whose father, Prince Alfred, was the second son of the late Queen Victoria.

PALACE COUP

The February Revolution was, in effect, a palace coup, engineered by the Tsar's own relatives, working closely with the British Embassy. Maurice

Paléologue, the French ambassador, called this aspect of the Revolution the "conspiracy of the Grand Dukes."[128]

British ambassador George Buchanan was directly involved in the machinations surrounding the Tsar's abdication. On March 14, Buchanan met with the Grand Duke Michael Alexandrovich, the Tsar's brother, and second in line to the throne. They discussed plans to force concessions from the Emperor.

Prime Minister Rodzianko was planning to meet the Emperor when he arrived by train that evening, and would request the Tsar's signature on a manifesto granting a constitution to the Russian people. This manifesto would make Nicholas II a constitutional monarch, ending the 1,000-year Russian autocracy.[129] But it would allow Nicholas to stay on the throne. The manifesto had been written by Grand Duke Paul Alexandrovich—Princess Paley's husband—with help from a lawyer. It had already been signed by Grand Dukes Paul, Michael and Cyril.[130] The only thing left was to obtain the Tsar's signature.

KING GEORGE V ENDORSES THE REVOLUTION

During their meeting of March 14, Grand Duke Michael asked Buchanan if he had "anything special" he would like to convey to the Emperor. Buchanan states in his memoirs:

> "I replied that I would only ask him to beseech the Emperor, in the name of King George, who had such a warm affection for His Majesty, to sign the manifesto, to show himself to his people, and to effect a complete reconciliation with them."[131]

Given the gravity of the situation, it seems improbable that Buchanan would have spoken "in the name of King George," without first getting the

King's approval. For that reason, it does not seem unwarranted to conclude that King George V of England—through his ambassador George Buchanan—intentionally and officially endorsed the Russian Revolution, on the night of March 14, while it was still in progress.

WHO GAVE THE ORDER?

There is some mystery as to why the Tsar ended up abdicating, rather than signing the manifesto creating a constitutional monarchy. Buchanan states in his memoirs that fate took a hand. The Tsar never saw the manifesto, he implies, because the Emperor's train never arrived that evening. In what appears to have been a carefully planned move, workmen had sabotaged the tracks ahead of the Tsar's train, so that Nicholas had been forced to divert to Pskov, the headquarters of General Russky, commander of the northern front.

According to Buchanan, the Tsar telegraphed Rodzianko from Pskov the next day (March 15), finally agreeing to the Duma's demand for a constitution. But Rodzianko told him, "Too late." Abdication was now the only course left.[132]

Why did Rodzianko change his mind? Buchanan says Rodzianko's hands were tied. The demand for abdication supposedly came from the Petrograd Soviet, a group of socialist agitators who had suddenly announced their existence on March 12, claiming to represent the workers and soldiers of Petrograd, but with no legal authority to do so.

"[W]hile I was talking with the Grand Duke the proposed manifesto was vetoed by the Soviet, and the abdication of the Emperor decided," Buchanan writes in his memoir.[133] There is a problem with Buchanan's story, however. Rodzianko did not take orders from the Soviet. He took orders from Buchanan.

"Dictator" of Russia

Let us recall Princess Paley's accusation that certain liberal politicians used to meet at the British embassy to plot revolution, among them, "Prince Lvoff, Miliukoff, Rodzianko, Maklakoff, Guchkoff, etc.."[134] These are the same men who forced the Tsar to abdicate on March 15, 1917. They are also the same men appointed that day to high positions in Rodzianko's Provisional Government. Prince Georgy Lvov was named Prime Minister, Pavel Milyukov Foreign Minister, Alexander Guchkov Minister of War, and Vasily Maklakov legal commissar.

Throughout the night of the coup, British Ambassador George Buchanan was at the center of events. Following the Tsar's abdication, on the evening of March 15, Buchanan was seen leaving the Winter Palace. Recognizing Buchanan as a friend of the Revolution, the mob "greeted him with loud cheers and escorted him back to the [British] Embassy, where they gave a rousing demonstration in honour of the Allies," reported *The Times* of London.[135] On March 24, 1917—nine days after the Tsar's abdication—a Danish newspaper correspondent reported that Buchanan now wielded the power of a "dictator" in Russia. He wrote:

> "England's domination over the [Russian] government is complete and the mightiest man in the empire is Sir George W. Buchanan, the British ambassador. This astute diplomat actually plays the role of a dictator in the country to which he is accredited. The Russian government does not dare to undertake any step without consulting him first, and his orders are always obeyed, even if they concern internal affairs. ... When Parliament is in session he is always to be found in the imperial box, which has been placed at his

disposal, and the party leaders come to him for advice and orders. His appearance invariably is the signal for an ovation."[136]

The imperial box which had been "placed" at Buchanan's "disposal," according to this report, was formerly reserved for the Emperor himself. Given the facts—at least as presented in this Danish newspaper account—we must regard with some skepticism Buchanan's claim that the Petrograd Soviet, during its three-day existence, had somehow acquired more authority than Buchanan to tell Rodzianko what to do.

CHAPTER 19

UNDERMINING RUSSIAN "DEMOCRACY"

T HE BRITISH PRESS made no effort to conceal its glee over the Tsar's downfall. On the contrary, British journalists implied that the Tsar had gotten what he deserved, for failing to heed Lord Milner's warning. "Every effort was shattered by the obduracy of the Tsar," reported the London *Guardian* on March 16, 1917. "It is noteworthy that the outbreak [of the Revolution] followed promptly on Lord Milner's return from Russia, where his failure was generally understood to mean that nothing could be hoped from the Tsar, and that the people must seek their own redemption."[137]

Of course, not everyone in Britain was pleased with Milner's Russian intervention. Laurence Ginnell, an Irish member of the House of Commons, spoke openly against it. On March 22, 1917, while the House of Commons composed a message of congratulation to the Russian Duma, Ginnell pointed out the hypocrisy of congratulating Russian rebels while hanging Irish ones. He sarcastically suggested the following wording for the message:

"[T]his House, while appreciating Lord Milner's action in fomenting the Revolution which has dethroned our Imperial Russian Ally... and having betrayed its own promise of self-government to Ireland, suspends its judgment on the new institutions alleged to have been founded in Russia until time has revealed their character."[138]

Ginnell's suggested wording was shot down as "irrelevant" and "negative," but, significantly, no one challenged his contention that Milner had instigated the Russian Revolution.[139]

CELEBRATING THE TSAR'S DOWNFALL

On March 22, 1917—with the Tsar and his family under arrest, and their fate uncertain—Great Britain granted recognition to the revolutionary government. Prime Minister David Lloyd George sent a telegram that day to Prince Lvov, Russia's new Prime Minister, stating:

"It is with sentiments of the most profound satisfaction that the peoples of Great Britain and the British dominions have learned that their great ally, Russia, now stands with the nations which base their institutions upon responsible government. ... I believe that the revolution... reveals the fundamental truth that this war is at the bottom a struggle for popular government and for liberty."[140]

That same day, former Prime Minister Herbert Henry Asquith declared in the House of Commons, "Russia takes her place by the side of the great democracies of the world. ... We... feel it our privilege to be among the first to rejoice in her emancipation and welcome her into the fellowship of free peoples."[141]

The British press hastened to assure its readers that Russia's new Provisional Government would stay in the war. There would be no separate peace with Germany. Milyukov made this clear at a March 23 press conference. "We shall remain faithful to all past alliances … " he said. "[I]t is Russia's duty to continue the struggle… for her own liberty, and for that of all Europe… Henceforward all rumours of a separate peace must vanish once and for all … "[142]

Britain's Hidden Agenda

"My only thought was how to keep Russia in the war," Buchanan later stated in his memoir. By the time he wrote these words in 1923, the public mood had changed. The murder of the Tsar and his family had horrified the world, as had the so-called "Red Terror," the bloody purge carried out by the Cheka, the Bolshevik secret police. Buchanan was now under fire for his role in the Tsar's overthrow. He invariably offered the same explanation to all his critics. Tsar Nicholas was wavering, Buchanan explained. The Emperor was considering separate peace with Germany. For the sake of the Allied cause, he had to be stopped.

Buchanan argued that the British Embassy had no choice but to support the Revolution. He wrote in his memoir: "It was Hugh Walpole, the head of our propaganda bureau, who… begged me to show by the warmth of my language at some public meetings where I had to speak that I was wholeheartedly on the side of the revolution. I accordingly did so. But if I spoke with emotion of Russia's new-won liberty… it was to render more palatable my subsequent appeal for the maintenance of discipline in the army, and for fighting, instead of fraternizing with, the Germans. My only thought was how to keep Russia in the war."[143]

Keeping Russia in the war certainly made sense, from the standpoint of British self-interest. But was that really Buchanan's goal?

"[W]E SHALL... SEE A SERIES OF REVOLUTIONS AND COUNTER-REVOLUTIONS..."

In a letter to Lord Milner of April 10, 1917, Buchanan admitted that he did not believe Russia would be of any further use in the war. He wrote:

> "The military outlook is most discouraging and I, personally, have abandoned all hope of a successful Russian offensive this spring. Nor do I take an optimistic view of the immediate future of this country. Russia is not ripe for a purely democratic form of government, and for the next few years we shall probably see a series of revolutions and counter-revolutions... A vast Empire like this, with all its different races, will not long hold together under a Republic. Disintegration will, in my opinion, sooner or later set in..."[144]

Why, then, had Britain supported the Revolution? If keeping Russia in the war was never a realistic hope, what was it all for? One is left to wonder whether the real point of Buchanan's intrigues was simply to make sure that Russia lost the war—as Lord Kitchener intended from the beginning— and to make sure that the Russian Empire never again rose to challenge Britain for "supremacy in the world," as Queen Victoria had once put it. Considered in this light, it begins to make sense why the British began plotting against the Provisional Government almost as soon as the Tsar was out of the way.

"Disintegration"

The practical effect of Britain's Russia policy in 1917 was to ensure the very outcome Buchanan predicted—"revolutions," "counter-revolutions" and "disintegration" for many years to come. Perhaps this was intentional.

On July 1, 1917, the Provisional Government kept its promise to the British to launch a major offensive. General Brusilov attacked the Austrians in Galicia. But his offensive collapsed in three days. More than 400,000 Russian soldiers were killed, wounded, or captured. An equal number deserted.[145]

The Brusilov offensive effectively ended Russia's experiment with democracy, as Ambassador Buchanan had predicted. Recall that, in his April 10 letter to Lord Milner, Buchanan admitted that he had "abandoned all hope of a successful Russian offensive..." and had predicted that Russian democracy would fail.[146] I do not believe that the accuracy of Buchanan's predictions was due to clairvoyance, nor to any special talent or insight on his part. Buchanan knew what was coming because he was personally involved in making it happen.

As a direct result of Buchanan's machinations, the Russian army was now in a state of full mutiny. From July 16-30, the streets of Petrograd were filled with armed, violent soldiers, sailors and workers, demanding an end to the war. This mutiny came to be known as the "July Days." Prince Lvov resigned as Prime Minister on July 20, replaced by Alexander Kerensky, a socialist.

The Kornilov Coup

On September 10, 1917, the Russian commander-in-chief Lavr Kornilov declared himself dictator and attempted to overthrow Kerensky's Provisional Government.[147] Kerensky accused the British of instigating the coup. Much evidence suggests he was right. On August 15, Buchanan wrote in his diary, "General Korniloff is the only man strong enough" to restore discipline in the army.[148] On September 8, Buchanan wrote further, "I do not regard Kerensky as an ideal Prime Minister, and, in spite of the services which he has rendered in the past, he has almost played his part."[149]

The coup broke out on September 10. Kornilov sent General Krymov to Petrograd with a large force, on the pretext of putting down a Bolshevik uprising. Krymov's true mission, however, was to overthrow Kerensky. In his 1927 memoir, *The Catastrophe*, Kerensky accused the British—and Lord Milner, in particular—of supporting the coup. Kerensky wrote:

"On the streets of Moscow pamphlets were being distributed, entitled 'Korniloff, the National Hero.' These pamphlets were printed at the expense of the British Military Mission and had been brought to Moscow from the British Embassy in Petrograd in the railway carriage of General Knox, British military attache. At about this time, Aladin, a former labor member of the Duma, arrived from England... [and] brought to General Korniloff a letter from Lord Milner, British War Minister, expressing his approval of a military dictatorship in Russia and giving his blessing to the enterprise. This letter naturally served to encourage the conspirators greatly."[150]

The British also provided Kornilov with an armored car unit, manned by British soldiers in Russian uniforms, and led by Lieutenant Commander Oliver Locker-Lampson.[151]

The coup failed, but it fatally weakened Kerensky's government, paving the way for the Bolsheviks. Perhaps that was its real purpose.

CHAPTER 20

LEON TROTSKY, BRITISH AGENT

A T THIS POINT, the strange figure of Leon Trotsky re-emerges. Trotsky had been arrested by Kerensky's Provisional Government in the aftermath of the "July Days" mutiny. However, on September 17—forty days after Kornilov's attempted coup—Kerensky decided to release Trotsky from prison. For the second time in five months, Trotsky had been set free just when the Revolution needed him.[152]

Upon his release, Trotsky took charge of the Bolshevik resistance. He was elected Chairman of the Petrograd Soviet on October 8. Two days later, on October 10, Trotsky led the Soviet in a vote for armed revolution. It was therefore no surprise when, on the night of November 6-7, 1917, Trotsky made his move, leading the Bolsheviks in a successful coup. Stalin acknowledged Trotsky's leading role in the coup, in a *Pravda* article of November 6, 1918. Stalin wrote:

"All practical work in connection with the organization of the uprising was done under the immediate direction of comrade Trotsky, the president of the Petrograd Soviet. It can be stated with certainty that the party is indebted primarily and principally to comrade Trotsky for the rapid going over of the garrison to the side of the Soviet and the efficient manner in which the work of the Military-Revolutionary Committee was organized ... "[153]

On March 14, 1918, Trotsky was appointed People's Commissar of Army and Navy Affairs, making him, effectively, commander-in-chief of the Red Army and Red Fleet.[154]

The Vietnam Before Vietnam

What happened next is one of history's great riddles—the inscrutable mystery of the Russian Civil War. On the night of November 6-7, 1917, the Bolsheviks seized Petrograd. But the vast Russian Empire remained unconquered. It took five years and more than 10 million dead for the Red Army to subdue the rest of the country.[155]

At the height of the Russian Civil War, in December 1918, more than 300,000 White Russian troops, supported by over 180,000 Allied troops (including 60,000 British), faced a Red Army of about 300,000. The Reds were surrounded, boxed into a small area around Moscow and Petrograd, and cut off from supply lines. "On every front, the Bolsheviks were being pressed back toward Moscow," writes Martin Gilbert in *World in Torment* (1975).[156] Moreover, the commander of the Bolshevik forces, Trotsky, had no military experience or training whatsoever.

How did the Bolsheviks manage to win? Russia could be called the Vietnam before Vietnam, a nation that fell to Communist rule, not because the Communist forces were stronger, but because the anti-Communist forces were betrayed.

When Princess Paley wrote her 1924 memoir, the fighting had not yet stopped in Russia. The last scattered bands of anti-Bolshevik guerrillas were still being hunted down in Central Asia. The Princess wrote, "Is it not to Great Britain that we owe the continuation of the Russian agony? Great Britain supports wittingly… the Government of the Soviets, so as not to allow the real Russia, the National Russia, to come to life again and raise itself up."[157] Was the Princess right? Did the Red Army and the "Government of the Soviets" prevail due to British support? Considerable evidence suggests that they did.

OPPOSITION TO RUSSIAN NATIONALISTS

Prime Minister David Lloyd George never wanted to fight the Bolsheviks, according to British historian Martin Gilbert in his 1975 book, *World in Torment: Winston S. Churchill 1917-1922*.[158] In Lloyd George's view, Britain's real fight in Russia was against the nationalists and monarchists.

There were practical reasons for this policy. In 1917, high-ranking British statesmen were pursuing plans to carve up the Russian Empire into a patchwork of buffer states and to bring the oil-rich Caucasus under British control. Lord Milner even considered dividing up Russia's territories with Germany.

The White Russian commanders, on the other hand, were nationalists. They would never agree to break up the Empire. Nor did they wish to bring back the liberal Duma which had started the revolution, in the first place. Most favored a temporary military dictatorship, followed by the eventual restoration of the Romanovs as constitutional monarchs.[159] These policies were unacceptable to Lloyd George. Consequently, the White commanders and their British sponsors could never agree on essential war goals.

What doomed the White armies, in the end, was their near-total dependence on Britain for funding, supplies, munitions, and military advisors.

They could not make a move without permission from the British War Office.[160] When the British finally cut off supplies and funding, the White armies were finished.

THE MYTH OF ALLIED INTERVENTION

During the Russian Civil War, more than 200,000 foreign troops were deployed on Russian soil. These included 60,000 British troops, as well as various numbers of Americans, Japanese, French, Czechs, Serbs, Greeks, Italians, and others.[161]

Soviet propaganda promoted the myth for 70 years that the "imperialist" nations of the world had ganged up on Russia to crush the Bolshevik Revolution. But that was never their mission. Had the Allies wished to drive out the Bolsheviks, they could have done so easily. The British sent troops to Russia—and persuaded other countries to do so—not to fight Bolshevism, but to pursue other objectives.

As long as Germany remained in the war, Britain's first priority was to try to restore an eastern front, to fight the Germans. Secondly, the British sought to help separatist movements form independent buffer states, especially in Finland, Poland, the Baltics and the oil-rich Caucasus region, thus weakening Russia and making it easier for Britain to exert control over the region.[162]

The Allies, in fact, did very little fighting in Russia, and not always against the Bolsheviks. When they helped the White armies, it was only in situations where White operations happened to coincide with other Allied objectives.

Indeed, it is a little-known fact that the first Allied troops to land in Russia were a contingent of British Royal Marines who ended up fighting alongside the Red Guards to defeat a force of anti-Bolshevik Finns. Trotsky himself had requested the British intervention.

Trotsky's Telegram

Murmansk was a vital Arctic seaport which had been Russia's lifeline throughout the war. On March 1, 1918, Trotsky sent a telegram to the commander of the Murmansk Soviet, Alexei Mikhailovich Yuryev. The telegram stated (falsely) that peace talks with the Germans had "apparently broken off" and ordered Yuryev to "protect the Murmansk Railway." Trotsky expressly ordered Yuryev to "accept any and all assistance from the Allied missions," by which he meant military assistance.[163] Trotsky thus ordered Yuryev to cooperate with the British fleet.

Why did Trotsky send such an order? The official story is that Trotsky had somehow been misled into thinking the peace talks had fallen through, for which reason he feared an imminent German attack on Murmansk. But, as Commissar of Foreign Affairs, Trotsky was in charge of the peace talks, and surely knew they were nearing a successful completion.[164]

Trotsky's claim that the peace talks had "broken off" was a false alarm. The real problem was the peace treaty itself. The Treaty of Brest-Litovsk ceded vast Russian territories to Germany. A German occupation force would be moving in quickly to claim them. Large stores of British supplies and munitions were stored at Murmansk. The British did not want these falling into German hands, nor into the hands of any German allies, such as the Finnish White Guards.

Most likely, this was the real reason Trotsky sent his March 1 telegram, instructing Yuryev to cooperate with the Allies. He did it to help the British.[165] Trotsky thus found himself, once again, in his familiar role of helping advance British interests, while claiming to champion proletarian internationalism.

Helping the Reds

The British needed a pretext for occupying Murmansk. Trotsky provided it. But he did so discreetly. Rather than contacting the British directly,

Trotsky used Commander Yuryev to make the request.[166] Trotsky's telegram to Yuryev, instructing him to allow the British fleet to land, would later be used against Trotsky as evidence in his 1937 treason trial.[167] The astonishing fact is that Trotsky singlehandedly legitimized Allied intervention in Russia, arranging for the British to receive a formal invitation from a Bolshevik official, Yuryev.

The first British troops landed at Murmansk on March 6, 1918.[168] They fought their first battle on May 2, fighting *for* the Bolsheviks, not against them. Finnish White Guards had captured the nearby town of Pechenga. It was feared they might be acting as a vanguard for the Germans. From May 2-10, the Royal Marines fought shoulder-to-shoulder with the Red Guards, driving the Finns out of Pechenga.[169]

CHAPTER 21

LETTING TROTSKY WIN

W INSTON CHURCHILL IS not the hero of this story. Far from it. But, in the bewildering muddle of the Russian Civil War, Churchill stands out, almost uniquely, as a voice of clarity and reason. He understood, from the beginning, that the Bolsheviks lacked popular support, and would likely collapse in the face of quick and decisive opposition. Unfortunately, Churchill was never allowed to organize such opposition.

At a War Cabinet meeting of December 31, 1918, Churchill proposed using military force to compel the Bolsheviks to hold a General Election overseen by the Allies. He was certain they would lose.[170] Lloyd George opposed this idea, as, indeed, he opposed any plan that stood a chance of toppling the Bolsheviks.

"LG [Lloyd George] is opposed to knocking out Bolshevism," wrote Sir Henry Wilson in his diary, after meeting with the Prime Minister on January 12, 1919. Wilson was Lloyd George's top military advisor.[171] After dining with Churchill on January 20, Wilson wrote, "Winston all against Bolshevism, & therefore, in this, against LG."[172]

No Support for "Reactionaries"

Martin Gilbert argues convincingly in *World in Torment* (1975) that Winston Churchill used all his power as War Secretary to fight the Bolsheviks, sincerely trying to defeat them. I have no reason to doubt this. Had Churchill been free to act, it seems likely he would have saved Russia from 70 years of Communism. But Lloyd George blocked him at every turn.

The Prime Minister used the same argument against the White Russians that he had previously used against the Tsar. He claimed the Whites were "reactionary" and that helping them would undermine Britain's commitment to "democracy," "self-determination of peoples" and other high ideals. Thus, when Churchill telegraphed Lloyd George on May 5, 1919, requesting urgent help for Admiral Kolchak's march on Moscow, the Prime Minister replied that he had no intention of helping Kolchak establish "a reactionary military regime" in Russia.[173]

To put it another way, Lloyd George demanded of Kolchak what no one demanded of the Bolsheviks—a commitment to liberal democracy. Churchill was therefore obliged to demand from Kolchak binding promises to appoint a democratically-elected constituent assembly; to grant independence to Poland and Finland; and to submit to the League of Nations the question of independence for other breakaway Russian provinces, such as Estonia, Livonia, Latvia, Lithuania, Georgia and Azerbaijan.[174] Not surprisingly, Kolchak refused these conditions.[175]

Words vs. Actions

Later, when General Denikin was advancing on Moscow from the south, Lloyd George once more interfered. Churchill was then trying to provide much-needed funding to Denikin, by giving him commercial loans and opening up trade with areas under Denikin's control. Lloyd George nixed this plan at a War Cabinet meeting of July 25, 1919, stating that he was not at all sure "Denikin and the officers with him were going to play the game."[176] The Prime Minister noted that Denikin was "surrounded by persons of reactionary tendencies," some of whom wanted to restore "a Czarist regime."[177] Lloyd George made clear, on that occasion, that he opposed restoring the Russian monarchy, even in a "milder," constitutional form.[178]

This anti-monarchical stance seemingly contradicted an earlier statement Lloyd George had made to his War Cabinet on July 22, 1918. At that time, the Prime Minister had said the "Russian nation should have the right of setting up any Government they chose. If they chose a Republican Government, or a Bolshevist Government, or a Monarchical Government, it was no concern of ours…"[179]

Consistency was never a strong point for Lloyd George, especially where Russia was concerned. But on one issue he was perfectly consistent, from the beginning. Lloyd George favored the Bolsheviks over any other faction contending for power in Russia.

"AT WAR" BUT NOT MAKING WAR

On July 4, 1919, as White General Nikolai Yudenich drew close to Petrograd, it was proposed at a cabinet meeting to provide British naval support via the Baltic Sea and the Gulf of Finland. Lloyd George refused. He said that, while Britain was technically "at war with the Bolsheviks," it was his policy "not to make war," for which reason he could not approve any naval attack on Petrograd.[180] With those words, Lloyd George neatly summarized Britain's overall policy toward the Russian Civil War, which was "not to make war."

The British malaise infected every allied army in the expeditionary force, including the Americans. Some 13,000 US troops were deployed in Russia in 1918-1919, of whom 344 died, and 125 were left behind. Most Americans never understood why they were there.[181] "What is the policy of our nation toward Russia?" asked Senator Hiram Johnson of California, in a speech of December 12, 1918. "I do not know our policy, and I know no other man who knows our policy."[182]

Lieutenant John Cudahy of the US 339th regiment, deployed to Russia in 1919, later wrote that, when the last American troops evacuated the Russian port of Archangel on June 15, 1919, "not a soldier knew, not even vaguely, why he had fought or why he was going now, and why his comrades were left behind—so many of them beneath the wooden crosses."[183]

FOR WHOM THE BELL TOLLS

The last British troops withdrew from Russia in October 1919.[184] The French and British governments cut off all aid to the White Russian forces on December 12, 1919, declaring they would no longer provide "assistance to the anti-Bolshevik elements in Russia, whether in the form of troops, war material or financial aid..."[185]

General Kolchak was betrayed and turned over to the Bolsheviks, shot before dawn on February 7, 1920—barely 24 hours before Churchill's article appeared in the *Illustrated Sunday Herald*.[186] General Wrangel—the last White commander with a substantial army—evacuated Russia on November 14, 1920.[187] Scattered bands of rebels continued fighting well into 1924, but with no chance of victory. Wrangel's withdrawal ended any hope of ousting the Bolsheviks.

On March 16, 1921, the British signed an Anglo-Soviet Trade Agreement with the Bolsheviks. On March 21, 1921, the Bolshevik government adopted the so-called New Economic Policy (NEP) reintroducing limited capitalism into Russia, and inviting foreign investment. On February 1, 1924, Great Britain formally recognized the new Union of Soviet Socialist Republics. As with so many wars in our modern age, millions were left to wonder what it had really been about.

TROTSKY'S SECRET

Leon Trotsky, at least, never entertained such doubts. His narcissism would not allow it. While living in exile in Mexico City, Trotsky wrote a "Testament" on February 27, 1940, reflecting on his stormy legacy. Trotsky wrote:

> "If I had to begin all over again I would of course try to avoid this or that mistake, but the main course of my life would remain unchanged. I shall die a proletarian revolutionist, a Marxist, a dialectical materialist, and, consequently, an irreconcilable atheist. My faith in the communist future of mankind is not less ardent, indeed it is firmer today, than it was in the days of my youth."[188]

We can assume then, that Trotsky, at least, died happy. On August 20, 1940, an agent of the Soviet secret police attacked Trotsky with an ice axe, a mountaineer's tool with a pick on one side and a flat adze on the other. The Spanish-born assassin, Ramón Mercader, buried the adze nearly three inches deep in Trotsky's skull.[189]

Trotsky's wife of 37 years, Natalia Sedova, had stayed with him till the end. It is reported that Trotsky and Natalya suffered a "serious marital rift" in Mexico, and that one of their quarrels concerned Trotsky's long-ago affair with British spy Clare Sheridan, cousin of Winston Churchill, as related in *Trotsky: A Biography* (2009) by Robert Service.[190] Whatever the ultimate truth may be regarding Trotsky's dealings with British intelligence, he took that secret to his grave.

THE COVER-UP

At this point, most readers will have realized that the rise of communism has been misrepresented in our history books. The proven involvement of Britain's secret services in both the French and Russian Revolutions raises questions as to whether either of those revolutions could have succeeded without British help. This raises a further question. If it is true that revolutions can succeed only with covert support from state security services—and assuming that professional revolutionaries are aware of this fact—it seems reasonable to ask whether any subversive movement would ever dare to attempt a revolution, without the hidden support of interested governments, such as that of Great Britain.

It is often said that Richard Nixon's downfall came not so much from the Watergate break-in, as from the cover-up afterwards. The same could be said of the British security services, whose role in fomenting the French and Russian Revolutions is slowly coming to light. The cover-up required extensive rewriting of history in a manner so brazen the deception could not be sustained. It is a testament to the skill and influence of Britain's information warriors that they managed to keep this secret so long. But the secret is out now. In the next section, I will focus on the cover-up, in which the full force of Britain's war propaganda apparatus was mobilized to deflect blame for these revolutions away from Great Britain and onto others, especially the Jews.

PART VI

THE COVER-UP

CHAPTER 22

BLAMING THE GERMANS

THE BRITISH PROPAGANDA offensive of 1919-1920 was overseen by the same people who had destabilized Russia in the first place. In short, the perpetrators were put in charge of the cover-up. Led by Britain's former ambassador to Petrograd George Buchanan, a tight group of "wartime propaganda specialists" (Alan Sarjeant's term, in his 2021 study *The Protocols Matrix*) set to work cleaning up the mess, crafting an approved, sanitized version of the Russian Revolution for use by future historians. These specialists were, in Sarjeant's words, "the very men who had formed the backbone of the British Russian Bureau that had worked so closely and so diligently alongside Military Intelligence in Petrograd during the war."[191]

As discussed in Chapter 1, Buchanan's dream team of wartime propagandists focused mostly on shifting blame to the Jews. But they did not target Jews exclusively. Germans were also blamed for funding and supporting the Bolshevik Revolution. Indeed, Jews and Germans were accused of working together in a nefarious alliance that purportedly dated back to the reign of Frederick the Great, in the 18th century.

The German connection was a crucial detail that made the whole story plausible. Most intelligent observers understood that a band of intellectual misfits like the Bolsheviks possessed neither the money, the power, nor the skill to overthrow a great empire like Russia's. Without help from some great power, such as Germany, the Bolsheviks would have spent their lives bickering in coffeeshops. British propagandists therefore made a special point of emphasizing Germany's sponsorship of the Bolsheviks.

CHURCHILL ACCUSES GERMANY

"How was Russia struck down? ... " asked Winston Churchill in the House of Commons, on November 5, 1919. "Lenin was sent into Russia by the Germans in the same way that you might send a phial containing a culture of typhoid or of cholera to be poured into the water supply of a great city, and it worked with amazing accuracy."[192]

Churchill was here referring to Germany's role in smuggling Lenin and other top Bolsheviks into Russia in 1917. Immediately following the Tsar's abdication, the Germans had transported a party of 32 Bolsheviks, including Lenin, from Zurich to Petrograd, by special train. Arriving in the Russian capital on April 16, 1917, Lenin immediately began organizing the Bolshevik Revolution, with financial and other support from the German government.

BOLSHEVISM INFECTS GERMANY

Why had the Germans done this? They claimed it was a military operation to destabilize Russia and hasten her surrender. On that level, the plan worked. Once installed, the Bolshevik government did its job, surrendering to Germany on March 3, 1918. In the process, the Bolsheviks gave up huge tracts of territory, including Finland, Poland, Ukraine, and the Baltic States. However, Germany's victory proved costly, as more than a million

German troops were now needed to occupy the territories newly ceded by Russia. These troops were desperately needed on the Western Front, but instead found themselves bogged down in a disintegrating Russian Empire that was rapidly descending into civil war.

Even worse, German troops fraternized with the Russians, becoming infected with their Bolshevik propaganda. This led to the German Revolution of 1918-1919, in which workers' and soldiers' councils sprang up all over Germany, modeled after those in Russia. The Kaiser was forced to abdicate and flee the country. Communist militias took to the streets. Bolshevik leaders such as Rosa Luxemburg and Karl Radek arrived from Russia to help lead the revolt. Parts of Germany broke away, forming Soviet states. The rebellion was put down only through bloody action by the German army and by war veterans organized in militias.

General Erich Ludendorff—who commanded German forces jointly with Field Marshall Paul von Hindernberg—admitted in his 1919 memoir that supporting the Bolsheviks had been a mistake. The Bolsheviks caused a domino effect that toppled both Russian and German governments. "By sending Lenin to Russia," he wrote sheepishly, "our Government had moreover assumed a great responsibility. From a military point of view his journey was justified, for Russia had to be laid low. But our Government should have seen to it that we also were not involved in her fall."[193]

PARVUS, BRITISH AGENT?

Who was responsible for this mistake? Who persuaded the German government to back the Bolsheviks? In fact, the author of this plan was very likely a British agent. He was Alexander Helphand (better known by his alias Parvus), a Russian-born Jew with close connections to British intelligence.

Born Israel Lazarevich Gelfand in what is now Belarus, Parvus left Russia at age 20, one step ahead of the secret police, who had marked him as a subversive. Parvus lived in Switzerland and Germany for some years, becoming a prominent figure among revolutionary exiles. He collaborated closely with Leon Trotsky, helping him formulate the doctrine of "permanent revolution." Trotsky admired Parvus for his keen mind, but later wrote, "there was always something… unreliable about Parvus. In addition to all his other ambitions, this revolutionary was torn by an amazing desire to get rich."[194]

ARMS DEALER FOR VICKERS

Parvus achieved his dream of wealth by selling arms in the Balkan Wars of 1912-1913, acting as a sales agent for the German Krupp conglomerate and the British firm Vickers. Parvus's partner in these endeavors was Basil Zaharoff (aka Basileos Zakarios), a Greek industrialist and high-level British agent who has been called the "guiding genius" of Vickers.[195]

Zaharoff helped build Vickers into a global powerhouse, acquiring for the British armament company the Maxim machine gun, the Nordenfeldt submarine, and other lucrative properties. He became the company's top international salesman, a leading stockholder, and one of the wealthiest men in Europe. During World War I, Zaharoff was "an Allied agent working at the highest levels," as even the *Encyclopedia Britannica* admits.[196] He was named a Knight Grand Cross of the Order of the British Empire in 1918, an honor not normally bestowed on foreigners.

DOUBLE AGENT

Most historians identify Parvus as a German agent. Without a doubt, he performed services for German intelligence.[197] However, he also made himself useful to Britain's secret services, through his work with Zaharoff and Vickers. Parvus's true and ultimate loyalty remains a matter of debate. In their book *Prolonging the Agony* (2017), authors Jim MacGregor and Gerry Docherty conclude that Parvus was a British asset. They write:

> "Parvus had spent a great deal of time in Germany since the early 1900s and was considered by many, including the German authorities themselves, to be a loyal German agent. Judging by his activities, however, from the time he moved to Constantinople in 1908 there can be little doubt that he was a double agent working for the British, or, to be more precise, the Rothschilds."[198]

Tellingly, Parvus's greatest intelligence coup—tricking the Germans into supporting the Bolshevik Revolution—turned out to be a disaster for Germany, but a great help to Britain. Perhaps that was the plan. As Ludendorff later admitted, the subversive influences unleashed by the Bolshevik Revolution directly caused the German government to collapse in 1918 (with considerable help from British intelligence, which supported the German rebels).[199] Thus, the Bolshevik triumph allowed Britain to achieve two objectives, ensuring that neither Germany nor Russia emerged victorious from the war. From the standpoint of *cui bono* (who benefits), the scales lean heavily toward the conclusion that Parvus was a British agent.

CHAPTER 23

WHY THE GERMANS
HELPED LENIN

F ROM A PRACTICAL standpoint, it was never in Germany's interest to overthrow the Russian government, or to plunge Russia into civil war. Chaos in the East would only distract from Germany's war efforts in the West. For that reason, German diplomats preferred making a separate peace with the Tsar, as they had been trying to do since late 1914. However, the British forced their hand, pushing Germany into a disastrous decision to support the Bolsheviks.

Upon hearing of Germany's peace offers to Russia, the British took three actions. First, they promised Constantinople to the Russians, as an inducement to keep fighting (see Chapter 8). Second, they instructed British ambassador George Buchanan to sabotage the peace party in Russia. This was accomplished partly by assassinating the "mad monk" Rasputin, who had been an influential voice for peace at the Russian court. Finally, it appears that the British dispatched double agent Parvus to trick the Germans into abandoning their peace talks with Russia, and to opt instead for toppling the Russian government—an extreme policy which the Germans had not previously pursued. In his 2005 book *Conjuring Hitler: How Britain and America Made the Third Reich*, Guido Giacomo Preparata describes the strategy of Parvus's British controllers. He writes:

> "It was precisely these separate negotiations between the German and Russian empires that Parvus was expected to sabotage. Until the last stages of the Bolshevik seizure of power, Helphand's chief assignment would be to steer the Germans so as to ruin their chances of communication with the czarist empire. While the hired assassins of Rasputin and the British ambassador Buchanan, supported by a team of professional spies sent from London, burned the bridges from St. Petersburg to Germany, Parvus et. al. burned those from Berlin to Russia."[200]

SECRET PLAN FOR REVOLUTION

On January 7, 1915, Parvus met with Freiherr von Wangenheim, the German ambassador to Constantinople, telling him, "The interests of the German government are identical with those of the Russian revolutionaries." He convinced Wangenheim that Germany would never be secure unless the Tsar was overthrown and his empire split into many parts. Germany should therefore support separatist and revolutionary movements in Russia, Parvus argued.[201]

The next day, Wangenheim sent a telegram to his Foreign Ministry, reminding them that Parvus had performed "useful services" for Gernany in the past, and urging his superiors to consider Parvus's plan. Helphand accordingly met with diplomats at the German Foreign Ministry sometime in February. He followed up with a 20-page memorandum dated March 9, 1915, in which Parvus laid out a detailed plan for the destruction and dismemberment of the Russian Empire. The key to Parvus's plan was that Germany should give full support to Lenin and the Bolsheviks. The Germans agreed to this.[202]

"From the middle of March, 1915, Helphand became the leading advisor to the German government on revolutionary affairs in Russia," write Parvus biographers Zeman and Scharlau in *The Merchant of Revolution* (1965). "His assignment was to organize a united front of European socialism against the Tsarist regime, and to enable the socialist party organizations in Russia to promote their country's collapse, through defeatist propaganda, strikes, and sabotage."[203]

Parvus was likewise put in charge of laundering money for these operations. The German Foreign Ministry paid out an estimated nine tons of gold over the next two years to fund Parvus's destabilization campaign, all of it processed through Parvus's elaborate network of international business and banking connections.[204]

If indeed Parvus was a British agent—as his close association with Zaharoff and Vickers suggests—then he was surely one of the slyest in the annals of British spycraft. In the end, Parvus successfully conned the German government into footing the bill not only for toppling the Tsar but for deposing the German Kaiser as well.

FINGER-POINTING

The machinations of Parvus led to much finger-pointing after the war. In 1923, the London *Morning Post* hosted a written debate between Nesta Webster—a leading British writer—and Kurt Kerlen, a German spokesman for General Ludendorff. Webster accused the Germans of having caused the Bolshevik Revolution by funding and supporting Lenin. Kerlen retorted that England had done as much as Germany to stir up revolution in Russia, and had drawn more benefit from it. "All is fair in love and war...," Kerlen wrote. "Decidedly Mrs. Webster's country has acted according to this rule, and the final result has proved fully in England's favour." Kerlen continued in these words:

"Lenin was allowed to pass through Germany. Trotsky was permitted to leave America, and when duly imprisoned in Halifax, was released and proceeded to Russia. If Ludendorff confesses frankly his share in sending Lenin to Russia, why do those who are responsible for Trotsky's journey not say openly what were their reasons?"[205]

Webster did not answer Kerlen's question. She could not. The German had opened a can of worms which the British establishment preferred to keep closed. The fact is, Germany and Britain had both supported the Bolsheviks. But there was a difference. Russia and Germany had been enemies. Russia and Britain had supposedly been allies. Germany's operation had been an act of war, Britain's an act of betrayal. More to the point, as Kerlen noted, the "final result" had "proved fully in England's favour."

CHAPTER 24

THE GERMAN ILLUMINATI

B UCHANAN AND HIS propagandists successfully rewrote the history of the
Russian Revolution. By 1920, the doctored story had congealed into
the form that most people recognize today. The revolution was portrayed
as a popular uprising of the Russian people against a cruel and incom-
petent Tsar. The revolution was just, but it was hijacked by Bolsheviks,
said Buchanan's propagandists. And who were these Bolsheviks? A cabal
of half-mad Jewish radicals propped up by German spymasters. This was
the story as Buchanan told it, and it is more or less the same story told to
this day.

Buchanan's propagandists had been successful, but their work was not
yet complete. As previously noted, Winston Churchill's February 8, 1920
article not only accused Jews of fomenting the Russian Revolution, but
also of secretly orchestrating "every subversive movement" in Europe,
as far back as Adam Weishaupt's Bavarian Illuminati and the French
Revolution of 1789.[206] This too was an essential part of Britain's post-
war propaganda narrative, every bit as crucial as the falsification of more
recent events. "Who controls the past controls the future," wrote George
Orwell in *Nineteen Eighty-Four*.

FALSIFYING HISTORY

In Chapters 9 and 10, I suggested that Churchill's claim of a 150-year conspiracy of Jewish subversion was a cover story calculated to deflect attention from Britain's own role as the chief funder and instigator of revolutionary movements during that era. As with the Bolshevik Revolution, Churchill and his colleagues did not exclusively blame the Jews, in this matter. They also accused Germany, and the Prussian monarchy, in particular.

In this, Churchill followed a well-trodden path. British intelligence operatives have been engaged, for more than 200 years, in a sustained effort to seed the historical record with doctored narratives alleging an alliance between Jewish and German occultists, organized in secret societies, and united for the common purpose of overthrowing Christian civilization.

According to this theory, German Illuminati infiltrated Masonic lodges in France and Germany during the 18th century, infecting them with Satanic doctrines (later portrayed as Jewish doctrines) which would ultimately evolve into communism. This is the "Judeo-Masonic" theory of communist origins, an idea which would later figure prominently in Nazi and Fascist ideology.[207] The degree to which British intelligence services contributed to the formulation of this theory is a topic most historians have neglected.

BRITISH INFLUENCE ON NAZI IDEOLOGY

As discussed in Chapters 11 and 12, the seedbed of communism was neither France nor Germany. It was the City of London Tavern in Bishopsgate. There, the London Revolution Society—a hotbed of British intelligence activity—plotted the French Revolution and oversaw the creation of the famous Jacobin clubs. It was from these Jacobin Clubs that a radical network would arise that would ultimately bring forth the Reign of Terror and the first recognizably communist movement, led by French revolutionary Gracchus Babeuf, whose connections with Britain's secret services we explored in Chapter 12.

Secret societies played a role in the French Revolution, to be sure. Their role was central. But the allegation that those societies were mainly under German or German-Jewish influence—the Judeo-Masonic theory—appears to be a misdirection. Great Britain was the number one enemy of France, during this era, and all evidence suggests that British influence over the Jacobin Clubs—and on the Masonic lodges that supported them—was overwhelming and decisive. Whatever the original reason may have been for this misdirection, it had unfortunate results. The worldwide dissemination of the Judeo-Masonic theory by Winston Churchill in 1920—five years before Hitler wrote on that same subject in *Mein Kampf*—clearly contributed to the early formation of Nazi ideology, at a time when the fate of the German nation still hung in the balance, and the German people still had options for moving in different directions.

WHO SERVES WHOM?

The essential claim of the Judeo-Masonic theory is that Jews created Freemasonry and Illuminism—or, alternatively, that Jews infiltrated these groups and took control of them—in order to use these secret societies as fronts for subversive activity. From the standpoint of propaganda, the purpose of this narrative was to portray Jews as the masterminds of the communist movement while portraying non-Jewish collaborators—specifically, Freemasons and Illuminists—as nothing more than useful idiots.[208]

My own research suggests that exactly the opposite is true. Much

evidence suggests that stories of a Judeo-Masonic conspiracy were deliberately planted by British agents, in order to deflect blame onto Jews for
subversive activities which the British themselves had carried out.

In the aforementioned article of February 8, 1920, Winston Churchill
used historical claims about a Judeo-Masonic conspiracy for just this
purpose, to support his contention that Jews were the most obvious sus-
pects for masterminding the Bolshevik Revolution. Churchill cited as his
source for this historical information one Nesta Helen Webster, whom I
mentioned in the last chapter. Webster's popular 1919 book *The French
Revolution: A Study in Democracy* alleged that a cabal of German Freemasons
and Illuminati had staged the French Revolution.[209] In subsequent writings, Webster would flesh out her theory by assigning ever greater por-
tions of blame to the Jews.

NESTA HELEN WEBSTER: PROPAGANDA ASSET

A good deal of circumstantial evidence suggests that Webster was a propaganda asset for the British government, and that her books were carefully contrived intelligence products. Webster's father Robert Bevan was
the head of Barclays Bank, making him one of the most powerful men
in the British Empire.[210] Her brother Edwyn Bevan was a high-ranking
intelligence officer, specializing in propaganda. During World War I, he
served in the small inner circle that ran Britain's War Propaganda Bureau
(known as Wellington House).[211] After the war, Bevan joined the Political
Intelligence Department of the Foreign Office.[212]

Given her family connections, it is not surprising that Webster's work
got a respectful reception from top publishers, newspaper editors, and
cabinet-level ministers such as Winston Churchill. Her books—especially *The French Revolution* (1919), *The World Revolution* (1921), and *Secret*

RICHARD POE

Societies and Subversive Movements (1924)—were extremely popular and helped bring the Judeo-Masonic conspiracy to a mainstream audience.

Webster's allegation of a centuries-old conspiracy of Germans, Jews, Jesuits, and Freemasons provided a useful counter-narrative for concealing British complicity in the Russian Revolution and in the long series of subversive movements which preceded it. Webster's narrative had the added advantage of vilifying the Germans, a high priority for British propagandists at the time.

That Webster accomplished her mission so capably is a testament not only to her talents, which were considerable, but to the patient groundwork laid by earlier writers on whom she relied. The story Webster told had been more than a century in the making, shaped and sculpted, through several generations, by the skilled hands of British intelligence operatives. Long before Webster was born, her predecessors had been hard at work perfecting this narrative, consciously designing it for the very purpose to which Webster now applied it.

MASONIC LODGES CORRUPTED

In her 1921 book *World Revolution: The Plot Against Civilisation*, Webster argues that a cabal of German occultists—the Illuminati—worked with Jewish allies to infiltrate and corrupt Freemasonry from within. By the late 18th century, she says, this cabal had transformed Europe's Masonic lodges into snakepits of revolutionary intrigue.

In keeping with her propagandistic mission, Webster took care to distinguish between English and "Continental" Freemasonry. The Continental lodges were corrupt, she said. English Freemasonry, on the other hand, was pure, unsullied, and blameless. Webster hammered this point hard, and for good reason. Freemasonry was widely perceived to be of English

— 116 —

origin. The Grand Lodge of London had unique authority to "recognize" other Grand Lodges abroad. For that reason, any attack on Freemasonry could easily implicate the "Mother Lodge" in London.

ENGLISH LODGES ABSOLVED

Mindful of the Mother Lodge's delicate position, Webster went to great lengths to assure her readers that the English lodges had never been subverted by Illuminist or Jewish infiltrators. On this point, she quotes John Robison, a British Freemason who had written on this subject in 1797. She writes:

> "These subversive theories emanated from certain secret societies of which an English writer calling himself John Robison described the aims in the title of his book, *Proofs of a Conspiracy against all the Religions and Governments of Europe carried on in the Secret Meetings of the Free-Masons, Illuminati, and Reading Societies*. Robison, who was himself a genuine Freemason, made a tour of the Continental lodges, where he found that a new and spurious form of masonry had sprung into existence. Both in France and Germany [Robison wrote] 'the lodges had become the haunts of many projectors and fanatics, both in science, in religion, and in politics, who had availed themselves of the secrecy and freedom of speech maintained in these meetings … . In their hands Freemasonry became a thing totally unlike, and almost in direct opposition to, the system imported from England, where the rule was observed that nothing touching religion or government shall ever be spoken of in the lodges.'"[213]

Webster thus exonerated the English lodges not only of any guilt in the French Revolution, but of any possibility of involvement in any other political intrigues. With this sweeping absolution, Webster performed a great service for English Freemasonry. But she didn't stop there. Like her predecessor John Robison, Webster went out of her way to vilify the German lodges.

JEWS AND PRUSSIANS IN COLLUSION

Webster claimed that the French lodges had once been as virtuous as the British ones, until they were corrupted by their German brethren. She thus identified Germany as the original source of the revolutionary contagion. In support of this claim, Webster quotes one Quintin Craufurd, a wealthy Scot who had served the British East India Company for twenty years, making his fortune in India, before showing up at the French court, where he became a friend and confidant of Marie Antoinette. Craufurd is known to have been a British secret agent.

In a 1794 letter, Craufurd informed Prime Minister William Pitt that the "diabolical doctrines" of the French Jacobins "were carried from Germany," specifically, from the "lodges of the German Freemasons and Illuminati..." and that the Revolution itself had been planned three years in advance "at a great meeting of Freemasons" in the German city of Frankfurt-am-Main.[214] Crauford thus distinguished himself as one of the earliest in a long line of British intelligence operatives to identify Germany as the source of revolutionary subversion.

More than a hundred years later, Webster expanded on Crauford's thesis by claiming that the German occultists who planned the French Revolution were assisted by Jews, whose "power... over the people was immensely increased by the overthrow of the [French] monarchy and aristocracy," according to Webster.[215] She further claimed that Jews had formed an alliance with the Prussian monarchy "from the time of Frederick the Great," serving as "Prussia's most faithful and efficient agents."[216]

BRITISH INTELLIGENCE PRODUCT

To a striking degree, the stories that Webster recycled and promoted in her books had been planted in the historical record by people—such as Quintin Craufurd—who are known to have been agents of the British secret services. In many cases, the stories they circulated were true or partly true, but they exhibited a persistent and predictable bias, having been skewed in such a way as to deflect attention from British intelligence operations, while shifting blame onto others.

In the 1790s, the British government faced a problem similar to the one it confronted after the Russian Revolution. The British needed to cover their tracks. As previously discussed in Chapter 11, British involvement in the French Revolution and the Reign of Terror was a poorly-kept secret, known to many prominent people, including Thomas Jefferson and the Marquis de Lafayette. Just as with Russia later on, the British government pretended to be horrified by the French Reign of Terror and by the murder of the French King and Queen. In reality, however, British agents had helped plan and instigate these very crimes. To conceal Britain's role in the bloodshed, it was necessary to construct a counter-narrative. This was done through the sponsorship and promotion of some of the early masterpieces of what we now call "conspiracy" literature.

CHAPTER 25

CONSTRUCTING THE JUDEO-
MASONIC CONSPIRACY

I N 1797, FRENCH Jesuit Abbé Augustin Barruel published a history of
the French Revolution, the first in what would become a five-volume
series. Intentionally or not, Barruel's history perfectly suited the needs of
British state propaganda. Titled *Memoirs Illustrating the History of Jacobinism
(1797-1800)*, Barruel's book blamed the French Revolution on a plot by
German Illuminists and German Freemasons, while pointedly absolving
English Freemasons from any role in the conspiracy. Not surprisingly,
Barruel's narrative relied extensively on material provided by British
sources, including known intelligence operatives.

The central ideas of Barruel's book—that the Bavarian Illuminati
were the hidden instigators of the French Revolution; that they aimed to
build a Satanic world order on the ruins of Christendom; and, finally, that
they disguised their Satanic agenda beneath a veneer of good intentions,
preaching liberty, equality, fraternity and the Rights of Man—all came
from British sources. Barruel's most important source was the aforementioned John Robison, a Scottish physicist, mathematician, and prominent

Freemason, who was writing a book on the same subject, and who generously shared his research with Barruel.[217] Robison, in turn, had gotten much of his material from one Alexander Horn, a Scottish Benedictine monk who happens to have been a British secret agent and diplomat.[218]

BRITISH INFLUENCE

Much of what Barruel wrote was true. Secret societies, with ties to the occult, had indeed played a significant role in the French Revolution. Many of the revolutionaries were, in fact, Freemasons, and had used Masonic lodges as cover for their secret meetings. But that was only half the story. Barruel failed to mention the crucial role of Britain's secret services in instigating the French Revolution, and manipulating the secret societies which took part in it.

Barruel's oversight was understandable. Like many French clerics, he had fled his native land to escape persecution, taking refuge in England. The British were his hosts and protectors. He was indebted to them. Moreover, as already mentioned, Barruel was largely dependent on British sources for his material.

He also enjoyed the favor of powerful factions in Britain, whose patronage he could not afford to lose. For instance, Barruel's work was warmly endorsed by Edmund Burke, the British statesman and philosopher now known as the "father of conservatism." Burke's 1790 book, *Reflections on the Revolution in France* had preceded Barruel's exposé by seven years, and had presciently condemned the French revolutionaries as destroyers of civilization, at a time when most Englishmen still saw them as champions of liberty. Burke read Barruel's book and, in a letter to Barruel of May 1, 1797, not only praised the book, but strongly endorsed its specific allegation of Masonic conspiracy, stating:

"I have known myself personally five of your principal Conspirators; and I can undertake to say from my own certain knowledge, that so far back as the year 1773 they were busy in the Plot you have so well described and in the manner and on the Principle which you have so truly presented. To this I can speak as a Witness."[219]

Burke recognized the propaganda value of Barruel's work, stating, "the great object of my Wishes is, that the Work should have a great circulation in France," for which purpose Burke offered financial support.[220] France was then still in chaos, its revolutionary government fighting off foreign interventions and uprisings by the hungry masses. Burke hoped the dissemination of Barruel's work in France would help further discredit the revolutionary regime, encouraging the rise of a conservative backlash.

ECHO CHAMBER

Published in London, Barruel's first volume became a world-wide bestseller. It made Barruel a rich man. His Scottish colleague Robison came out with a similar work shortly after, called *Proofs of a Conspiracy against all the Religions and Governments of Europe, Carried on in the Secret Meetings of Freemasons, Illuminati and Reading Societies.*[221] Robison's book quoted Barruel and promoted the French Jesuit's work.

Both books appeared the same year, 1797. Barruel and Robison thus formed a kind of echo chamber, both promoting the idea that the Bavarian Illuminati were the true culprits behind the French Revolution—an idea which seems to have come originally from British secret agent Alexander Horn.

To this day, the works of Barruel and Robison form the basis for most popular writings promoting Masonic theories of revolution. Surprisingly, though, Jews are hardly mentioned in either book. In 1797, the Jewish element had not yet been added to the story. This was a significant omission, considering the great importance assigned to Jews by later writers.

It was not until the 20th century that writers such as Nesta Webster and William Guy Carr solidified the Judeo-Masonic conspiracy in its final form, portraying Jews as the head of the snake. Both of these 20th-century writers had strong connections with British intelligence. The English-born Carr was a Canadian naval officer who served in the Canadian Intelligence Service during World War II, after which he embarked on a successful career as a conspiracy author.

But that is getting ahead of our story.

The Simonini Letter

For whatever reason, neither Barruel nor Robison had accused the Jews of playing any significant role in the French Revolution. Their Illuminist-Masonic theory was not yet a Judeo-Masonic theory. That would soon change.

In 1806, a man identifying himself as Jean Baptiste Simonini wrote Barruel to inform him that, although he had done well in exposing "the hellish sects which are preparing the way for Antichrist," he had overlooked the role of "the Judaic sect."[222]

Simonini claimed to be an army officer of the Italian city of Florence. He claimed that he had learned from his own secret intelligence work that the Freemasons and Illuminati were founded by Jews, and acted as fronts for Jewish intrigue. Somewhat improbably, Simonini claimed that he had convinced a group of Piedmontese Jews that he too was Jewish, whereupon they had ostensibly opened their hearts to him and told him the whole plan.

Barruel tried to contact Simonini, but failed. To this day, no evidence can be found that such a person even existed. Simonini's original letter to Barruel has never been found. It seems likely that the author of the "Simonini" letter may not have been who he claimed to be. His true name, nationality, and motivation can only be guessed. I would not rule out the possibility that "Simonini" was yet another British intelligence asset—in the tradition of Quintin Craufurd and Alexander Horn—who sought, by his letter, to feed additional material to Barruel, hoping he would include it in his books.

THE WORLD JEWISH CONSPIRACY IS BORN

If Simonini was another British agent, he went further than his predecessors. He claimed that Jews sought to dominate the world, and had devised a practical plan for doing so. In his book *Warrant for Genocide*, Norman Cohn notes that the Simonini letter sets forth "in embryo" "the whole myth of the Judeo-Masonic conspiracy" which later swept Europe in the 20th century. Cohn summarizes Simonini's theory in these words:

> "The mysterious Simonini goes on to reveal… that the Order of the Freemasons and the Illuminati were both founded by Jews… [that] everywhere Jews were disguising themselves as Christians… [that] the Jews would buy up all lands and houses, until the Christians were completely dispossessed. Then the last stage of the plot would be carried out: the Jews 'promised themselves that in less than a century they would be masters of the world… and reduce the remaining Christians to a state of absolute slavery'. *Only one serious obstacle remained—the House of Bourbon, which was the Jews' worst enemy, and the Jews would annihilate that.* [emphasis added]"[223]

Whatever else can be said about Simonini's letter, it showed that forces had emerged by 1806 which sought to blame Jews specifically for the French Revolution, an agenda which had not been evident in earlier writings.[224] "Simonini" sought to persuade Barruel that Jews were mortal enemies of the French monarchy and the ultimate puppetmasters behind the murder of the King. This was a novel claim, and an unlikely one. It was the English—not the Jews—who had been almost constantly at war with France since the 12th century. The British Crown was, for that reason, a more likely suspect. Yet Simonini's story is the one that stuck. The reason, I believe, is that the British government wanted it to stick, and, through its capable secret services, had the means of bringing that about.

CHAPTER 26

DISRAELI'S PROPHECY

B ARRUEL AND ROBISON, with their respective books, had introduced the public to the Illuminati, and to the idea that Satanist followers of Adam Weishaupt had infiltrated Masonic lodges, using them as platforms to promote revolution. Significantly, however, neither book accused the Jews of any significant role in this conspiracy.

The book that finally brought the World Jewish Conspiracy to a mass audience was penned—somewhat surprisingly—by Benjamin Disraeli, who would later become Britain's first (and only) Prime Minister of Jewish origin (though he converted to Anglicanism at age 12). Disraeli entered the House of Commons in 1837, and became a leader of the Young England movement, pushing for a restoration of the aristocracy's ancient feudal privileges, even though he was not himself an aristocrat. Many of Disraeli's allies in Young England doubted his sincerity, seeing him as an opportunist and social climber, seeking to ingratiate himself with the titled classes, and so he may have been.[225]

Seen in this light, Disraeli's greatest act of sycophancy may have been writing a novel titled *Coningsby*, published in 1844. The novel promoted the ideas of Young England. It also featured a character named Sidonia, based upon the legendary financier Lionel Rothschild. Disraeli describes Sidonia in these words:

"Europe did require money, and Sidonia was ready to lend it to Europe. France wanted some; Austria more; Prussia a little; Russia a few millions. Sidonia could furnish them all... He was lord and master of the money market of the world, and of course virtually lord and master of everything else... Monarchs and ministers of all countries courted his advice and were guided by his suggestions."[226]

"...THE WORLD IS GOVERNED BY VERY DIFFERENT PERSONAGES..."

Elsewhere in the novel, Sidonia tells the character Coningsby how he traveled across Europe raising money for a Russian loan, finding, in each country he visited, that the ministers he dealt with were Jews. "So you see, my dear Coningsby, that the world is governed by very different personages from what is imagined by those who are not behind the scenes," Sidonia concluded. With these words, Disraeli gave his readers to understand that the world was literally "governed" by Jews. Why did he write this?

Perhaps more than any other work prior to the *Protocols of the Learned Elders of Zion*, Disraeli's novel *Coningsby* fueled speculation about the power of Jewish bankers to manipulate governments. Such speculation only intensified when Disraeli was appointed Prime Minister in 1868, then again in 1874. Queen Victoria ennobled him in 1878, naming him Earl of Beaconsfield. Disraeli's skyrocketing fortunes seemed to fulfill Sidonia's boasts of Jewish power, lending credence to everything Disraeli had written in *Coningsby*.

Disraeli Predicts the Rise of Communism

Disraeli went further. He accused his own people of being fomenters of revolution, in words that would not have been out of place in the Simonini letter. He wrote:

> "You never observe a great intellectual movement in Europe in which the Jews do not greatly participate. ... [T]hat mighty revolution which is at this moment preparing in Germany, and which will be in fact a second and greater Reformation, and of which so little is as yet known in England, is entirely developing under the auspices of Jews, who almost monopolise the professorial chairs of Germany."[227]

Disraeli thus appears to predict the emergence of German communism—also known as Marxism—four years in advance of the publication of the *Communist Manifesto* by Karl Marx and Friedrich Engels. How did he know? And why did he boast of it in public?

Conflicting Loyalties

"Why did Benjamin Disraeli, who was Jewish, write a novel about a Jewish banking conspiracy?" asks Dr. Stanley Monteith in his 2000 book *Brotherhood of Darkness*. Monteith draws a surprising conclusion.[228] He suggests that Disraeli's loyalty to the British Establishment outweighed his loyalty to his own Jewish people. Monteith suggests that Disraeli deliberately exposed Jews to vilification and suspicion, in order to serve what he deemed to be a higher master. Whoever that master may have been, he (or she) evidently had the power to reward Disraeli with the Prime Ministership of Great Britain and with an earldom.

— 128 —

I find Monteith's argument plausible. Indeed, it is difficult for me to conceive of any other explanation for Disraeli's indiscreet boasts of Jewish power in his novel *Coningsby*. To say these boasts were ill-advised is an understatement. They marked a decisive turning point in the mood and tenor of anti-Jewish writings. They also gave a much-needed boost to Britain's covert propaganda campaign to deflect attention away from British involvement in the French Revolution, and to implicate Jews instead. As a direct result of Disraeli's intervention, the Illuminist-Masonic conspiracy of Barruel and Robison suddenly transformed into the Judeo-Masonic conspiracy of Simonini.

Disraeli's personal responsibility for this innovation is confirmed by no less an authority than Nesta Webster. In her 1921 book *The World Revolution*, Webster writes, "Were the Jews concerned in the organization of Illuminism and its subsequent developments? At present this is not clearly proved." Disciples of Simonini, she argued, had failed to come forth with hard evidence, offering only "vague assertions" and rumors. Webster continues:

> "We should require more than such vague assertions to refute the evidence of men who, like Barruel and Robison, devoted exhaustive study to the subject and attributed the whole plan of the Illuminati and its fulfilment in the French Revolution to German brains. Neither Weishaupt, Knigge, nor any of the ostensible founders of Illuminism were Jews; moreover, as we have seen, Jews were excluded from the association except by special permission. None of the leading revolutionaries of France were Jews, nor were the members of the conspiracy of Babeuf."[229]

With these words, Webster dismissed Simonini's claims, insisting that the Illuminist conspiracy was originally a product of "German brains," not Jewish ones. Her opinion holds weight, since Churchill cited Webster by name as his primary authority for claiming a 150-year conspiracy encompassing "every subversive movement" in Europe. If indeed Jews were implicated in that conspiracy—and ultimately dominated it, as Churchill charged in his 1920 article—when did they achieve this dominance? When did it begin?

Webster implies that Jews became a significant force in subversive movements only sometime in the 1840s, and then only in Germany. As her source for this information, she cites Disraeli and Disraeli alone. Webster writes, "In Germany before 1848 Disraeli himself declared them [Jews] to be taking the lead in the revolutionary movement, and with the First Internationale they come forward into a blaze of light."[230]

A Blaze of Light

When Webster wrote that Jews had "come forward into a blaze of light" with the founding of the First International in 1864, she was referring principally to Karl Marx, who became the leader of that organization, mysteriously raised up by helping hands behind the scenes. Originally called the International Workingmen's Association, the First International was founded (ostensibly) by British and French trade union leaders in London on September 28, 1864. Marx did not speak at the first meeting, yet he quickly became the acknowledged leader of the movement, a position he held until it dissolved in 1872.

Marx's connection with the First International catapulted him to fame. In fulfillment of Disraeli's prophecy, a "Reformation" thus came out of Germany, led by a German Jew (albeit one who was raised Lutheran from age 7). There was something strangely contrived about the whole affair. Like Benjamin Disraeli, Marx had always managed to make himself useful to the British establishment, and he was never more useful than in his role as leader of the First International. It was there that Marx performed the valuable service of putting a Jewish face on a movement—the communist movement—which had not been notably Jewish in the past.[231]

CHAPTER 27

"THE TERRIBLE MARX"

W HEN THE INTERNATIONAL was founded in 1864, Marx was recognized almost instantly as its de facto leader. This was a little surprising, as Marx had previously been an obscure figure, mostly seen lurking in the Reading Room of the British Museum. He had not been a mover and shaker in the world of British trade unions. Yet now, quite suddenly, Marx was catapulted into the position of the world's most powerful voice for the international labor movement (or at least the appearance of such).[232]

Officially called the International Workingmen's Association (IWA), the International was supposed to function as a union without borders, bringing all workers of all countries under a single authority. In reality, it was a British organization serving British interests. Pulling strings behind the scenes was a small circle of liberal aristocrats imbued with the philosophy of Young England, whose example they followed by supporting the labor movement while working behind the scenes to keep it on a tight leash.

ARISTOCRATIC SUPPORT

One of these behind-the-scenes supporters was John Villiers Stuart Townshend, 5th Marquess Townshend, a British peer and Liberal Member of the House of Lords. When the International was formed, he moved it into offices at 18 Greek Street which already housed another organization, the Universal League for the Material Elevation of the Industrious Classes, founded and run by the Marquess. Most of the British members of the International's governing committee came from Townshend's Universal League, including George Odger, a London union leader who was widely touted as the driving force behind the International. In some respects, the International could be described as Townshend's Universal League wrapped in a new skin.[233]

When Marx received his invitation to take part in what would turn out to be the founding meeting of the International, he eagerly accepted, sensing that an important door had opened for him in the corridors of power. Marx biographer Rolf Hosfeld comments, "Though he had become accustomed to turning down such requests over the past ten years, Marx immediately agreed. This time, he informed Engels, he had the clear feeling that for the first time, real powers were in play…"[234]

Psychological Operation

Marx was right. "Real powers" were indeed in play. But they were not the powers of the revolutionary proletariat or even the British trade union movement. The International's precise relationship with the British Foreign Office is not clear, but there can be little question that the purpose of the new organization was to mobilize trade union support for British foreign policy objectives. Its initial assignment appears to have been to neutralize growing support for Abraham Lincoln among British workers.

On the surface, the British working man should have been expected to oppose Lincoln, out of his own economic interest. Lincoln's naval blockade of the South had cut off cotton supplies to British textile mills, causing massive unemployment. For that reason and others, the British government was pressing Lincoln hard to accept a peaceful separation of North and South. But Britain's working class did not support its government on this issue. English workers sided overwhelmingly with Lincoln, whom they saw as a crusader against slavery. This posed a problem for the British establishment.

RUSSIAN SUPPORT OF LINCOLN

The British government was in a delicate position. It had given its full and public support to the Confederacy. Indeed, Great Britain had helped instigate the Southern secession in the first place. Britain had long held a de facto monopoly on Southern cotton exports, 70 percent of which were purchased by Britain each year. The North had tried to replace England as the South's leading trade partner, by building its own cotton mills and imposing tariffs to block Southerners from trading with England. Britain took this as a threat to her vital interests. Her secret services went to work building a secessionist movement in the South.

Most historians agree that the Southern secession movement began with a July 2, 1827 speech by one Thomas Cooper of South Carolina. As it happens, Cooper was a British intelligence asset, born in Westminster, England and educated at Oxford. He was sent to Paris in 1792, where he helped the radical Jacobins sieze power and launch the Reign of Terror. In 1794, Cooper emigrated to South Carolina, became a judge, and used his position of influence to agitate for secession. Cooper is merely one in a wider network of British agents who sowed division in America prior to the Civil War.[235]

When war finally broke out on April 12, 1861, England and her French ally Napoleon III tried to strong-arm Lincoln into accepting Southern independence. But Lincoln refused. France and England decided to take naval action to break the Union blockade and force Lincoln to the bargaining table. Before they could act, however, the Russian Tsar Alexander II came to Lincoln's rescue. Two Russian fleets—almost the entire Russian navy—arrived in New York and San Francisco, in September and October 1863 respectively. They remained in US waters for seven months. Their presence discouraged the French and British from intervening, and probably saved the Union.[236]

REGAINING THE MORAL HIGH GROUND

Russian support for Lincoln had turned Britain's propaganda position upside down. Since 1807, the British had preened themselves as opponents of the slave trade, even while financing slavery in the American South. At the same time, the British had condemned Russia as a barbarous land which kept its people in serfdom. Now Alexander II had reversed all that. In 1861, he freed Russia's serfs. In the same year, Russia emerged as the only great power in Europe to support Lincoln in his fight against the Southern slave owners.

The International Workingmen's Association (IWA) appears to have been launched, at least partly, as a propaganda operation to reclaim the moral high ground for Britain. In January, 1863, Polish rebels launched an uprising against Russia, with covert British support. Russia responded with a bloody crackdown. On cue, French and British newspapers raised an outcry against Russian atrocities and agitated for Polish independence. Russia was now back on the defensive, on trial before the world as a brutal oppressor of its subjects.

COOPTING LINCOLN'S ENGLISH SUPPORTERS

Many historians hold that the International was founded, at least partly, to organize support among French and English workers for the hard-pressed

Polish freedom fighters.[237] This is partly true. In fact, a Polish nobleman, Prince Władysław Czartoryski helped pay travel costs for French delegates to attend the International's founding meeting in London. The Prince was an arch-conservative with no interest in labor organizing, but someone had evidently clued him in that the International served a larger purpose, that of supporting Poland's fight against Russia.[238]

At the same time, the International, under Marx's leadership, became a rallying point for working-class supporters of Lincoln. Marx is credited with heroically defying the British government by supporting the North in America's Civil War. However, the true effect of Marx's "support" proved harmful to Lincoln, not helpful. Marx effectively coopted Lincoln's supporters, by drawing them into an organization—the International—which was actively engaged in undermining Lincoln's staunchest ally, the Tsar. Intentionally or not, Marx diluted and neutralized the energy of Lincoln's supporters, by manipulating them into a position where the only practical way to support Lincoln was to sign on with the International and support its anti-Russian agenda as well. Marx may or may not have understood the nature of this deception, but, as usual, he followed orders and played his part well.

Anti-Russian Agitation

Under Marx's leadership, the International kept up a constant drumbeat of anti-Russian agitation for years. Not unlike Trotsky, who constantly claimed to be acting on behalf of the proletariat while serving British interests, Marx was adept at inventing high-sounding excuses for his pro-British stances. At times, however, the illusion wore thin, and Marx's voice resounded with the unmistakable tones of British Foreign Office propaganda. For instance, in an 1867 speech to the

International's General Council, Marx accused Russia of seeking "world domination" and demanded an independent Poland as a buffer against Russian aggression.

"In the first place the policy of Russia is changeless … ," said Marx. "Its methods, its tactics, its manoeuvres may change, but the polar star of its policy – world domination – is a fixed star. … There is but one alternative for Europe. Either Asiatic barbarism, under Muscovite direction… or else it must re-establish Poland, thus putting twenty million heroes between itself and Asia and gaining a breathing spell for the accomplishment of its social regeneration."[239]

Marx was never so passionate as when he was denouncing Russia's alleged designs for "world domination." On the issue of workers' rights, however, the International proved listless and ineffective. Marx's 1912 biographer John Spargo admitted that the International's fearsome reputation was largely illusory, and that it mainly functioned as a publicity platform for building the myth of what he called "the terrible Marx." Spargo observed:

> "As soon as workers went out on strike anywhere the International was blamed. It was said in the newspapers and widely believed, that the International was a secret conspiratory society, at the head of which was the terrible Marx, who had written a very wonderful book in mystic language only to be learned by the initiated. With millions of dollars at their disposal, the emissaries of this society plotted revolution and compelled innocent workers to go out on strike, sealing their lips with fear. As a matter of fact, the International was not in any manner connected with the majority of these strikes."[240]

Nonetheless, writes Spargo, this phantom organization provided the springboard for a "great international movement which would terrify half the governments of the world."[241] Perhaps that was its true purpose. Instead of making actual revolution, it generated fear of imaginary revolution. In this latter endeavor, it proved highly effective.

When the Paris Commune was declared on March 18, 1871—a revolutionary government formed in the turmoil of France's defeat in the Franco-Prussian War—all eyes turned to the "terrible Marx" and his International, who were believed to have instigated the uprising. In fact, Marx had opposed the insurrection from the beginning.

The Germans had captured the Emperor Napoleon III on September 1, 1870, ending the French monarchy. A Provisional Government was declared, but France descended into chaos, with conservatives in the countryside demanding a new king while city dwellers—especially Parisians—sought a republic. On September 9, 1870, Marx wrote a declaration for the International, warning the workers of Paris that any attempt to overthrow the Provisional Government "would be a hopeless piece of folly."[242] Marx biographer Max Beer writes, "Marx then urged the French workers not to do anything foolish, not to set up a revolutionary Commune of Paris, but to make use of their republican liberties to create proletarian organisations and to save and discipline their forces for future tasks." The Parisians ignored Marx and proclaimed the Paris Commune on March 18, 1871.[243]

At that point, Marx had no choice but to embrace the Commune or risk irrelevance. But his private views differed from his public ones. In an 1881 letter to a friend, Marx wrote, "[The Commune] was merely the rising of a town under exceptional conditions, the majority of the Commune was in no sense socialist, nor could it be."[244] Marx biographer

Spargo concurs, stating that the Commune was nothing more than "the revolt of a city of republicans against a nation of monarchists."[245]

Notwithstanding his private cynicism regarding the Commune, Marx publicly played the role of revolutionary firebrand. The violence and vandalism of the Communards—who had senselessly set fire to many public buildings—horrified all of Europe. Marx's apparent support of the Commune brought him and the International into disrepute. According to Spargo:

> "[T]he Commune was regarded as a blood orgy of revolutionary excesses, and the International was held to be responsible for all. When the General Council [of the International] issued the brilliant manifesto, *The Civil War in France*, which Marx wrote after the fall of the Commune, the English press bitterly denounced it as a shameful, 'treasonous publication,' and called upon the government to punish the signatories and to take special care to discover the 'cowardly anonymous author' and bring him to justice, whereupon Marx at once wrote to the London newspapers declaring himself the author of the manifesto."[246]

It was all posturing. The "terrible Marx" was an illusion. Marx did not, in fact, support the Commune. Nor did he suffer any serious persecution for pretending to support it. Marx's pamphlet, *The Civil War in France* was an anti-climax. It became, according to Spargo, "the swan song of Marx and of the first International."[247] The following year, the International split into factions, its power broken.

Yet Marx's legacy lives on. Of what, then, does his legacy consist? As noted in Chapter 17, Marx received unexpected praise from the British establishment in 1882, the last year of his life. That year, Alfred Milner and Arnold Toynbee, two young Oxford graduates, delivered two separate—but strangely similar—lecture series, on the topic of socialism. Both called Marx a genius. Both declared that socialism was Britain's secret weapon for heading off revolution. Both suggested that Marx was on the right track, but hinted that he may have gone too far, in his pursuit of communism. "[P]ure Communism" might be "impracticable" for the present age, said Milner.[248]

What then was Marx's contribution? In their 1882 lectures, Toynbee and Milner both strongly implied that Marx's true value to the British Empire may have lain precisely in his tendency to push things too far, to play the role of the "terrible Marx." By raising the threat of bloody revolution, they implied, Marx had frightened the bourgeoisie into accepting more moderate forms of socialism. And, as discussed in Chapter 17, the specific forms of socialism Toynbee and Milner approved were those which would protect, rather than threaten, the position of Britain's ancient aristocracy, in accordance with the agenda of Young England.

CHAPTER 28

THE SUPER-CAPITALIST
CONSPIRACY

I N THE PRECEDING pages, I have argued that Marxism ultimately did not oppose the interests of the great imperial powers, but rather served those
powers, especially England. Some readers may find this farfetched. But it
did not seem farfetched to Nesta Webster and her respected colleagues at
elite British newspapers in the early 1920s. In fact, their view of Marxism is
not much different from mine, except that I see Marxism (and its offspring
Bolshevism) as having served primarily British interests, while Webster and
her colleagues thought the Bolsheviks served German interests.

Webster, in fact, argued that communism was a capitalist plot. She accused "super-capitalists" of deliberately creating Bolshevism as a strategy
to line their pockets. Its purpose, she said, was to trick workers into giving
up their rights and accepting a slave-like status, whereby their only choice
was to "work or starve."[249] The true purpose of Bolshevism, she wrote,
was to allow "the industrial exploitation of Russia by the German and
Jewish Company of super-Capitalists, whose real schemes were camou-
flaged under the guise of Communism…"[250]

RUSSIA ENSLAVED

Who were these super-capitalists? Webster said they were industrialists and bankers whose investments in Bolshevik Russia had made them hidden masters of the country. She wrote:

> "The plan of Germany and her Jewish allies has succeeded admirably. The Russian owners of land and property have been dispossessed, Russian industry has been wrecked, the Russian workers have been reduced to a condition so abject that they are ready to work for any master who will only give them bread…"

Webster was not alone in believing that German and Jewish "super-capitalists" secretly controlled Bolshevik Russia. That view was widely shared by Webster's colleagues in the right-leaning press, and apparently encouraged by the British government, or at least elements thereof. The British press, at that time, was still strictly controlled by the propaganda apparatus set up during the war. The "super-capitalist" theory would not have received such wide circulation unless it was approved by Britain's official organs of state propaganda.

PROJECTION?

Among those promoting the "super-capitalist" theory in the early '20s were such prominent opinion leaders as Wickham Steed, editor of *The Times* of London; H.A. Gwynne, editor of the London *Morning Post*, and Robert Wilton, who not only served as Petrograd correspondent for *The Times* but also as an agent of British military intelligence in Russia.[251] The super-capitalist theory was also popular in France, where journalist André Chéradame wrote:

"Bolshevism leads necessarily to the exploitation of Russia for the profit of a syndicate of super-capitalists of which the real leaders are Jews and Germans, that after the period of frightful licence which was necessary for the collapse of Russia, Russian workmen are now subjected to a régimé a hundred times more tyrannical than that of the Tzar."[252]

Webster and her colleagues were not off the mark in suggesting that certain "super-capitalists" profited from Bolshevism. However, they neglected to point out that the most lucrative post-revolutionary deal, to date, had been struck by a British company, Anglo-Persian Oil (now known as British Petroleum), as described in Chapter 9.

Quite possibly, the ruckus in the British press over "super-capitalist" exploitation may have been at least partly a case of projection, a classic propaganda ploy whereby you accuse your target of doing what you are actually doing. But Webster added a deeper dimension. She scrutinized the Bolshevik Revolution from an aristocratic perspective redolent of the Young England movement. Specifically, she argued that Bolshevism—and its evil twin "super-capitalism"—were products of bourgeois decadence, that is, products of a newly untrammeled middle class, no longer restrained by the nobler impulses of the aristocracy. In Webster's eyes, the Red Terror in Russia simply proved, once more, that efforts to improve upon the feudal order only ended up making things worse.

WAS WEBSTER A YOUNG ENGLANDER?

In her 1921 book *World Revolution*, Webster claims that the downfall of the French nobility removed the last institutional restraint on middle-class money-grubbing. This argument seems to place Webster squarely in the tradition of Young England—a movement, discussed in Chapter 15, which sought a return to feudalism, as a cure for modern ills. In support of her position, Webster cites Marx's famous passage on bourgeois revolution, wherein Marx states that the rise of the middle class "destroyed all feudal, patriarchal, and idyllic relations" between rich and poor, aristocrat and peasant, leaving only "self-interest," "callous cash payment," and "naked, shameless, direct, brutal exploitation." Webster writes:

> "Thus in the opinion of the leading prophet of modern Socialist thought, *it was the destruction of feudalism that led to the enslavement of the proletariat.* Exaggerated as this indictment of the *bourgeoisie* may be, there is a certain degree of truth in Marx's theory. The class that lives on inherited wealth is always the barrier to the exploitation of the workers. To the noble who paid 500 louis for his *carrosse*, or the duchess who never asked the price of her brocaded gown, where was the advantage of underpaying the dressmaker? ... [I]t is thus against 'the newly rich' that we find the bitterest complaints of the people directed."[253]

THE "SPIRIT OF THE JEW"

Webster went on to specify that the worst of the "newly rich" were Jews. Thus, the bourgeois spirit unleashed in the French Revolution was, at its root, "the spirit of the Jew," she said.[254] Webster wrote:

> "Under the monarchy the Jews had been held in check by laws limiting their activities, but the edicts passed at the beginning of the Revolution, decreeing their complete emancipation, had removed all restraints to their rapacity. ... [T]he abolition of feudalism has

led to the domination of the money-lender, and the money-lender is in most cases a Jew."[255]

Had he lived to read these words of Nesta Webster, Marx likely would have agreed with them. Marx did not spare his fellow Jews from the ideological condemnation he thought they deserved. In his 1844 pamphlet, "On the Jewish Question," Marx argues—very similarly to Nesta Webster—that "practical" Judaism is little more than "huckstering and money." To the extent that middle-class Christians of the industrial age had also become money-grubbers—that is, to the extent that "the practical Jewish spirit has become the practical spirit of the Christian nations"—Marx concluded that "the Christians have become Jews."[256]

Thus we have come full circle to the same, strange coincidence of interests that united Karl Marx and his aristocratic patron David Urquhart, the alliance between revolutionary and reactionary. Marx, Urquhart, and Webster all believed that the "abolition of feudalism" had created a soul-less, money-grubbing society, driven by what Webster called the "spirit of the Jew." From her vantage point in the early 20th century, Webster added the further observation that capitalism—unrestrained by the paternal impulses of the nobility—would lead inexorably to "super-capitalism" and its evil twin Bolshevism.

Webster implies that the restoration of feudalism might cure those ills. She was not the first to consider this possibility. That was certainly the solution offered by the Young England movement of the 1840s, and by its spiritual descendants through the years. A good deal of evidence suggests that a similar agenda still smolders in the hearts and minds of certain global leaders today. We will consider the evidence for this in the remaining chapters of this book.

PART VII

THE THIRD BRITISH EMPIRE

CHAPTER 29

THE ROUND TABLE

I N HIS NOVEL *Nineteen Eighty-Four*, George Orwell foretold a future in which the British Empire merges with the United States to form Oceania, a superstate driven by an evil ideology called Ingsoc (an abbreviation for English Socialism).[257] Orwell's dystopia was based on his knowledge of actual plans circulating among British elites.

Modern globalism—the drive to set up a single world government—was born in Victorian England. As British power expanded in the 19th century, global dominion seemed inevitable. Imperial administrators laid plans for a world united under British rule. The key to making it work was for Britain to join forces with the United States, just as Orwell described in his novel. Many Anglophiles in the US were eager to go along with this plan. "We are a part, and a great part, of the Greater Britain which seems so plainly destined to dominate this planet..." enthused *The New York Times* in 1897, on the occasion of Queen Victoria's Golden Jubilee.[258]

"FEDERATION OF THE WORLD"

In 1842, Alfred Tennyson—soon to become Queen Victoria's official poet laureate—wrote the poem "Locksley Hall." It envisioned a golden age of peace, under "universal law," a "Parliament of man" and a "Federation of the world."[259] Tennyson's words foreshadowed the League of Nations and the UN. But Tennyson did not invent these concepts. He merely celebrated plans already underway among British elites.

Generations of British globalists have cherished Tennyson's poem as if it were Holy Writ. Winston Churchill praised it in 1931 as "the most wonderful of all modern prophecies." He called the League of Nations a fulfillment of Tennyson's vision.[260]

LIBERAL IMPERIALISM

Another British leader influenced by Tennyson's poem was philosopher John Ruskin, previously mentioned in Chapter 16. In his first lecture at Oxford in 1870, Ruskin electrified students by declaring it was Britain's destiny to "Reign or Die"—to rule the world or be ruled by others.[261] With these words, Ruskin gave birth to a doctrine that would soon come to be known as "liberal imperialism"— the notion that "liberal" countries should conquer barbarous ones in order to spread "liberal" values.[262] A better name might be "socialist imperialism" as most of the people who promoted this concept were socialists, or at least claimed to be.

Ruskin called himself a "Communist," before Marx had finished writing *Das Kapital*.[263] In Ruskin's view, the British Empire was the perfect vehicle for spreading socialism. Ruskin's socialism was strangely mixed with elitism. He extolled the superiority of the "northern" races, by which he meant the Normans, Celts, Vikings, and Anglo-Saxons who built England. He saw the aristocracy— not the common people— as the embodiment of British virtue.[264] Ruskin was also an occultist and (according to some biographers) a pedophile.[265] In these respects, his eccentricities resembled those still fashionable in certain globalist circles today.

THE RHODES TRUST

Ruskin's teachings inspired a generation of British statesmen. One of the most devoted of Ruskin's followers was Cecil Rhodes (1853-1902). As an undergraduate, Rhodes heard Ruskin's inaugural lecture and wrote out a copy of it, which he kept for the rest of his life.[266]

As a statesman, Rhodes aggressively promoted British expansion. "The more of the world we inhabit, the better it is for the human race," he said.[267] In his will, Rhodes left a fortune to promote "British rule throughout the world"; federation of all English-speaking countries; and "the ultimate recovery of the United States of America as an integral part of the British Empire."[268] All of this was supposed to lead to "the foundation of so great a power as to hereafter render wars impossible and promote the best interests of humanity," Rhodes concluded in his will.[269] Thus, world peace would be attained through British hegemony. By the 1890s, most British leaders agreed with Rhodes.

SECRET SOCIETY

Rhodes' ideas were destined to change the British Empire. For that reason, it is important to understand the true source of his ideas. Rhodes was only 23 years old when he wrote his "Confession of Faith," an 1877 document which lays out his grandiose plans to expand British power. In that document, Rhodes declared his intention to form a secret society modeled after the Jesuits and Freemasons, but dedicated to what Rhodes considered a better purpose. He wrote, "Why should we not form a secret society with but one object, the furtherance of the British Empire and the bringing of the whole uncivilised world under British rule, for the recovery of the United States, for the making the Anglo-Saxon race but one Empire."[270]

It is remarkable that Rhodes managed to achieve so many of his aims.

He did, in fact, form a secret society—ostensibly in 1891—which all the best and brightest in the British Empire hastened to join. There is some dispute among historians as to what this society was originally called, or how exactly it was related to a tangle of other Ruskinite groups which formed around it. Most agree, however, that Rhodes' disciples (or, more accurately, Ruskin's disciples) eventually converged around a group called the Round Table. These Ruskinite groups ultimately succeeded in drawing the United States back into a sort of union with Great Britain, albeit covertly, in a manner so subtle few even noticed it was happening.

THE HIDDEN HAND OF THE ARISTOCRACY

Was Rhodes a genius then? If it were true that his prophetic vision of a world-ruling, English-speaking empire sprang unbidden from his 23-year-old brow, then Rhodes deserves to be numbered among the great world conquerors, in the company of Alexander, Napoleon, and Genghis Khan. Much evidence suggests, however, that Rhodes was merely a front for other interests, which included the British Crown and certain powerful, aristocratic families.

We know for a fact that one of Rhodes's original supporters was the Crown Prince Edward—later King Edward VII—whose business with the Rhodes group was often conducted through a trusted intermediary, Reginald Balliol Brett, Lord Esher.[271] We also know that the secretive network Rhodes founded got support from the aristocratic Cecil family. Readers may recall that "the Cecils and their relations" were accused of being the oligarchical power behind the British throne, in testimony before the US Senate, during the Versailles Treaty hearings of 1919, as related in Chapter 16. It therefore seems reasonable to assume that Rhodes's agenda was approved at the highest levels of the British establishment.

THE DOMINIONS

Following Rhodes's death in 1902, Alfred Milner took over his movement. This is the same Alfred Milner who would one day deliver Britain's final ultimatum to the Tsar, as described in Chapter 18. In keeping with Rhodes's vision, Milner set up secretive "Round Table" groups to propagandize for a worldwide federation of English-speaking countries.[272] In each target country— including the US— a separate Round Table group was formed, which recruited local leaders to act as Judas goats, leading their fellow countrymen to the proverbial slaughter. In fact, the Round Table was leading people to a literal slaughter. War with Germany was expected. The Round Table sought commitments from each English-speaking colony to send troops when the time came. Australia, Canada, New Zealand and South Africa agreed.[273]

Rhodes's English-speaking federation proved to be a harder sell in the colonies. The colonies wanted independence, not union. So the Round Tablers proposed a compromise. They offered "Dominion" status or partial independence instead. Canada was to be the model. It had gained Dominion status in 1867. This meant Canada governed itself internally, while Britain ran its foreign policy. Canadians remained subjects of the Crown. The same deal was now offered to other English-speaking colonies.[274]

The Round Tablers had to work quickly. War with Germany was coming. Britain needed to mollify the Dominions with self-rule, so they'd agree to provide troops in the coming war. Australia became a Dominion in 1901; New Zealand in 1907; and South Africa in 1910.[275]

COURTING THE UNITED STATES

The United States presented a special challenge. We had been independent since 1776. Moreover, our relations with Britain had been stormy, marred by a bloody Revolution, the War of 1812, border disputes with Canada, numerous trade wars and British-led banking crises, as well as British meddling in our Civil War.

Beginning in the 1890s, the British waged a public relations blitz called "The Great Rapprochement," promoting Anglo-American unity.[276] Scottish-born steel magnate Andrew Carnegie called openly for a "British-American Union," in 1893. He expressly advocated America's return to the British Empire.[277] British journalist William T. Stead argued in 1901 for an "English-speaking United States of the World."[278] Stead was another Ruskinite, one of the three original founders of Rhodes' secret society in 1891. The other two founders were Rhodes himself and Lord Esher, who represented the Crown.[279]

THE BURDEN OF EMPIRE

Great Britain sought union with the United States not out of goodwill, but necessity. As early as 1883, Cambridge historian John R. Seeley suggested that the cost of defending Britain's colonies might outweigh the benefit. Seeley was one of John Ruskin's original disciples (albeit from the Cambridge branch, not the Oxford one). His views were very much in line with the other Ruskinites.

In his 1883 book *The Expansion of England*, Seeley lamented the "great burden which is imposed by India" and suggested that "England would be better off now... had she remained standing, as a mere merchant, on the threshold of India, as she stands now on that of China."[280]

Seeley further warned that the British Empire now found itself sandwiched between "two gigantic neighbours in the West and East," the United States and Russia respectively, both of which were potential threats. These were empires of a new type, he said, "continuous land powers," concentrated in a single land-mass, and therefore efficient and cost-effective to defend. Britain's sprawling empire, by contrast, had "an ocean flowing through it in every direction, like a world-Venice, with the sea for streets," making it vulnerable and costly to defend. Clearly, the future belonged to the "continuous land powers" Seeley fretted.[281]

MERGING WITH AMERICA

In his 1901 book *The Americanization of the World*, William T. Stead argued that England had only two choices. She must *merge* with America or be *replaced* by her.[282] For committed imperialists like the Ruskinites, there was really no choice. Merging with the US might save Britain's place in the world. But competing with the US could only end in defeat.

British leaders knew that policing their Empire had become too costly. Granting self-rule to the Dominions saved some money, as the Dominions now paid for their own defense. But military spending was still too high. In 1906, British banker Lord Avebury warned that the financial burden of imperial defense had become critical. The US was getting rich at Britain's expense, he complained. While the US profited from the Pax Britannica, Britain spent 60 percent more than America on its military, to keep the world safe for business.[283] Something had to be done. It turned out that 23-year-old Cecil Rhodes had been right all along. The solution to Britain's problems lay in drawing the United States back into some kind of formal union with the British Empire.

CHAPTER 30

THE SPECIAL RELATIONSHIP

F ROM THE BRITISH standpoint, the Great Rapprochement was a flop. When Britain declared war on Germany in 1914, troops poured in from every corner of the Empire. But not from America. The US sent troops only in April 1917, after 2 ½ years of hard British lobbying. To the British, the delay was intolerable. It proved that Americans could not be trusted to make important decisions. The Round Table therefore sought a "Canadian" solution. It sought to manipulate the US into a Dominion-like arrangement, with Britain controlling our foreign policy. It took two world wars and tens of millions of deaths to accomplish this goal. Eventually, however, the British got what they wanted.

WAR TO END WAR

World War I pushed the world toward global government, giving rise to the League of Nations. This was by design. British design. Generations of schoolchildren have learned that Woodrow Wilson was the father of globalism. But Wilson's "ideals" were spoon-fed to him by British agents.

On August 14, 1914—only 10 days after England declared war—novelist H.G. Wells wrote an article headlined, "The War That Will End War."

"[T]his is now a war for peace … " he declared. "It aims at a settlement that shall stop this sort of thing for ever."[284] Wells released a book version of "The War That Will End War" in October 1914. He wrote, "If Liberals throughout the world … will insist upon a World conference at the end of this conflict … they may … set up a Peace League that will control the globe."[285] Wells did not invent the idea of a "Peace League." He was simply promoting official British policy. Wells was then a secret operative for Britain's War Propaganda Bureau (known as Wellington House).[286]

BRITISH AGENTS IN THE WHITE HOUSE

British leaders understood that their Peace League would never work without US support. For that reason, British intelligence made special efforts to penetrate the Wilson White House, which proved surprisingly easy.

Wilson's closest advisor was "Colonel" Edward House, a Texan with strong family ties to England. During the Civil War, House's British-born father made a fortune as a blockade runner, smuggling cotton to England, then returning with British munitions to arm rebel troops.[287] Young Edward House and his brothers attended English boarding schools, at the insistence of their father.[288] While advising President Wilson, Colonel House worked closely with British spies, including Sir William Wiseman, the US station chief for Britain's foreign intelligence service. House, Wiseman, and Wilson became intimate friends, even vacationing together.[289] This is the same William Wiseman who would later order Trotsky released from a Canadian internment camp so he could join the revolution in Russia, as described in Chapter 2.

The idea for a "League of Nations" came from Sir Edward Grey, Britain's Foreign Secretary. In a letter of September 22, 1915, Grey asked

Colonel House if the President could be persuaded to propose a League of Nations and pretend it was his idea. Grey felt the proposal would be better received coming from a US president. Grey wrote:

> "To me, the great object… is to get security for the future against aggressive war. How much are the United States prepared to do in this direction? Would the President propose that there should be a League of Nations… I cannot say which Governments would be prepared to accept such a proposal, but I am sure the Government of the United States is the only Government that could make it with effect. …"[290]

Colonel House persuaded Wilson to do it. When the President later attended the Paris Peace Conference in 1919, Wiseman and House were close at hand, guiding his every move, along with a bevy of other British and US officials, all committed to the Rhodes agenda, and many tied directly to Milner's Round Table.[291]

MISSION ACCOMPLISHED

John Bruce Lockhart, a former officer of Britain's Secret Intelligence Service (SIS), later called William Wiseman "the most successful 'agent of infuence' the British ever had."[292] British historian A.J.P. Taylor wrote that "He [Wiseman] and House made the 'special relationship' a reality."[293] To what were they referring?

Many historians hold that the US-UK "special relationship" began only after World War II, with the creation of NATO and the UN. However, Taylor correctly notes that the seeds of the "special relationship" were planted earlier, at the Paris Peace Conference of 1919. In Paris, US and UK officials secretly agreed to coordinate policy, so that both countries would act as one. Two think tanks were created to facilitate this, Chatham House (UK) and the Council on Foreign Relations (US).[294] It had to be done quietly, through back channels. Round Table operatives on the British side worked with a carefully hand-picked group of US Anglophiles (many of whom were also Round Table members).[295]

THE MECHANISM OF CONTROL

On May 30, 1919, the Anglo-American Institute of International Affairs (AAIIA) was formed, with branches in New York and London. A formal structure now existed for harmonizing US and UK policy at the highest level. However, the timing was bad. Anti-British feeling was rising in America. Many blamed England for dragging us into war. At the same time, English globalists were denouncing Americans as shirkers for failing to support the League of Nations. The US Senate had voted against joining on November 19, 1919. In view of these tensions, the Round Tablers decided to separate the New York and London branches in 1920, for appearances' sake.

Upon separation, the London branch was renamed the British Institute of International Affairs (BIIA). In 1926, the BIIA received a royal charter and became the Royal Institute of International Affairs (RIIA), commonly known as Chatham House. Meanwhile, the New York branch became the Council on Foreign Relations in 1921. After separating from Chatham House, the CFR continued working closely with its British counterpart, under a strict code of secrecy called "Chatham House rules."[296]

THE "REAL STATE DEPARTMENT"

The Council on Foreign Relations (CFR) allowed British elites to exert a powerful influence over our foreign policy, effectively transforming the

United States into a dominion of Great Britain, albeit secretly, out of sight of the public. Through the years, Washington insiders have come to refer to the CFR as the "real State Department."[297]

The establishment of the CFR was a great victory for the Round Table. But they were still far from their ultimate goal. The US Senate had delivered a harsh rebuff to the Round Tablers, by rejecting the League of Nations not once, but twice, on November 19, 1919, then again on March 19, 1920. This was a setback for British globalists, but they were patient and persistent. It took another World War— and the persuasive talents of Winston Churchill— to finally draw the US into global government, via NATO and the UN.

CHAPTER 31

WINSTON CHURCHILL, FATHER OF MODERN GLOBALISM

C HURCHILL'S VISION OF global government was oddly similar to that of Cecil Rhodes and the Round Table. Churchill called for a "world organisation" backed by a "special relationship" between English-speaking countries. On February 16, 1944, Churchill warned that, "unless Britain and the United States are joined in a Special Relationship ... within the ambit of a world organisation—another destructive war will come to pass."[298] Accordingly, the UN was founded on October 24, 1945.

However, the UN was not enough. Cecil Rhodes and the Round Table had always maintained that the true power behind any global government must be a union of English-speaking peoples. British journalist and states-man Norman Angell had clarified this principle in 1942, insisting that the coming world government must be led by a "nucleus of authority"— specifically by "the West"—which in turn must be led by "the English-speaking world."[299]

Churchill repeated this plan in his "Iron Curtain" speech of March 5, 1946 at Westminster College (Missouri). Churchill warned that the UN had no "international armed force" or atomic bombs. The US must therefore join with Britain and other English-speaking countries in a military alliance. No other force could stop the Soviets, said Churchill. He further stated that "world organisation" was useless without "the fraternal association of the English-speaking peoples. This means a special relationship between the British Commonwealth and Empire and the United States."[300]

Churchill's words led to the 1949 NATO Treaty and the "Five Eyes" agreement, pooling intelligence efforts by the US, UK, Canada, Australia and New Zealand. Step by step, we drew ever closer to the global super-state Orwell called Oceania.

A self-described "Tory anarchist," Orwell hated Soviet Communism. If he wished, he could have written *Nineteen Eighty-Four* as a sort of British *Red Dawn*, with England groaning under Soviet occupation. But that was not Orwell's message.[301] He was not warning of foreign invasion or infiltration. Orwell warned of a danger closer to home. He warned of British globalists and their plan for a union of English-speaking countries driven by what he called "Ingsoc" ideology. In many respects, the world we inhabit today is the world Orwell foresaw.

CHAPTER 32

TRIUMPH OF THE KING

I T IS SAID that history is written by the victors. Who, then, were the victors who wrote the history of World War I? For whose benefit was the story spun? An intriguing answer to this question can be found in the opening lines of *The Third British Empire* (1926) by Alfred Zimmern, one of the founding members of the British Round Table. Zimmern wrote:

> "In 1914 there were numbered among the world's sovereign states a British Empire, a German Empire, a Russian Empire, an Ottoman Empire, and an Austro-Hungarian Monarchy presided over by an Emperor. London, Berlin, St. Petersburg (as it was then still called), Constantinople, and Vienna were all centres of empire. To-day there is a German Republic, an Austrian Republic, a Turkish Republic, and a Federation of Republics on the old Russian soil. But there still remains a British Empire."[302]

In short, every great royal house in Europe had fallen, except Great Britain's. The British monarchy had defeated every rival. It had won for itself a supreme power which no earthly king had wielded before. Although

Zimmern does not quite put it this way, his words carry an implication that the true victor in World War I was King George V of England and the British ruling class generally. They won for the simple reason that they were the last ones standing.

YOUNG ENGLAND REVISITED

The victorious British monarchy now faced a problem, however. Through the subversive work of its intelligence services—as documented in this book—the British ruling class had spent more than a hundred years promoting intoxicating—indeed, revolutionary—ideas about liberty, fraternity, and equality. This genie would not go willingly back into its bottle. Having successfully overthrown so many empires, the newly radicalized masses would now turn their eyes toward Europe's last remaining empire and ask themselves why it still existed. In *The Third British Empire*, Zimmern posed the problem thus:

> "The questions to which we shall be seeking answers... are three in number. Firstly, *why* has the British Empire survived at a time when these other empires have dissolved and disappeared? Secondly, *how* has it survived? In what form has it survived? Thirdly, *what* must it do to justify its survival in an age which seems destined to dissolve empires?"

The problem then was how to justify the existence of the British Empire. To accomplish this, British elites turned to a familiar strategy which had worked well in the past, the strategy of Young England. The ruling classes would present themselves as the friends and benefactors of the people, the guardians of their rights and liberties. Through propaganda, new enemies would be created. The hostility of the masses would be turned elsewhere.

EMPIRE OF PEACE

In keeping with this plan, Zimmern declared the birth of a new British Empire, which he called the "Third British Empire." The first empire, he said, came to an end with America's Declaration of Independence in 1776. The second empire ended sometime between 1914 and 1926, said Zimmern.

Why those years in particular? The mere waging of World War I would not account for the end of the second empire. If colonies are the measure of an empire's strength, Britain was surely stronger after the Great War, for it gained many colonies in the peace settlement. In what way, then, did the war years mark such a critical turning point? Zimmern explains that the Round Table announced a new policy during the war. It recommended that the British Empire rebrand itself as a "Commonwealth of Nations." Zimmern further explains that the purpose of the new "Commonwealth" would no longer be to serve the interests of Great Britain, but rather to help guard the peace of the entire world. This would be done through a new institution called the League of Nations.

IMPERIALISM BY OTHER MEANS

When Zimmern wrote, the United States had already refused to join the League of Nations twice. But, as a Round Tabler, Zimmern understood the power of patience. He knew that plans were already afoot to bring the Yanks around. And he knew that Great Britain would proceed with her plans for global government in any case.

As Zimmern explained it, Great Britain was voluntarily giving up its global power. She had promised to grant self-rule to her colonies, as soon as they showed themselves ready for it. The British Navy would no longer serve as policeman for the world. Henceforth, the League of Nations would provide a system "fitted to replace that which passed away for Britain in 1914," Zimmern wrote.[303]

Behind these pretty words lurked a hard-nosed reality. British elites understood that the true purpose of the League of Nations was to expand British power, not diminish it. Some of the more idealistic US supporters of the League of Nations had discovered this while butting heads with their British counterparts. For instance, US socialist writer Charles Edward Russell, after dining with a group of prominent British newspaper editors, found that they were "obsessed with forming a permanent Anglo-American league to 'control the world," notes Susan Brewer in her 2019 book *To Win the Peace*.[304] As previously noted in Chapter 30, British novelist and propaganda asset H.G. Wells had admitted in 1914 that the purpose of the proposed "Peace League" was to "control the globe."[305] He later wrote, "The British Empire… had to be the precursor of a world-state or nothing…"[306]

WOLF IN SHEEP'S CLOTHING

Throughout World War I, the British War Propaganda Bureau unleashed a veritable army of propagandists on the United States, tasked with lobbying for a permanent Anglo-American military alliance, under the guise of a "League of Nations." One of these was Philip Whitwell Wilson, then US correspondent for the *London Times*. Following a speech by Wilson on April 22, 1918, the *Boston Globe* reported, "Britain Putting By Empire for Mankind: Glories of Conquest Yield to Service." The article explained:

> "Great Britain is done with the glories of empire and the future will see her in cooperation with America and the other democratic countries of the world, one of an international league of peace, backed up by an international army and navy, devoted to the service of mankind, according to Philip Whitwell Wilson…"[307]

Wilson was a wolf in sheep's clothing. The "peace" he offered was the same peace envisioned by Cecil Rhodes, which could only be attained through world conquest by a union of English-speaking nations. In this new arrangement, America would bear the greatest burden, as designated global policeman.

When Wilson gave this speech, World War I was still raging and the Russian Civil War was just getting started. More than 13,000 US troops would soon be deployed to Russia, for the ostensible purpose of fighting the Bolsheviks. Unbeknownst to his American hosts, Wilson had played a major role in helping Lenin gain power in the first place, and was thus largely responsible for the chaos in Russia which would soon take the lives of 344 American troops, not counting 125 who were left behind and never seen again. Wilson was, in fact, part of a secret team of British operatives who had spent 15 years grooming Lenin and other top Bolsheviks in London, prior to the outbreak of the Russian Revolution.

CHAPTER 33

LENIN IN LONDON

LENIN MADE SIX visits to London between 1902 and 1911.[308] Indeed, virtually all the top Bolshevik leaders would visit London during those same years, including Trotsky and Stalin. What were they doing there? British researcher Alan Sarjeant—the same Alan Sarjeant whose 2021 study *The Protocols Matrix* I cited in Chapter 1—has amassed considerable evidence that Bolshevik leaders were groomed in London by a network of influential people connected to British intelligence. One of these was the aforementioned Philip Whitwell Wilson.

In fact, Lenin actually stayed at Wilson's home at 16 Percy Circus on his second visit to London. Russia's 1905 Revolution was then in progress. Visiting Russian revolutionaries were closely watched by British authorities, who had a cooperative arrangement with the *Okhrana*, the Tsarist secret police. Despite Wilson's position as a respected writer for the *Daily News* and a candidate for public office (he would be elected to the House of Commons the following year, as a Liberal MP), Wilson thought nothing of risking his career by harboring a notorious Russian revolutionary in his own home, under an assumed name, right under the nose of the police. Sarjeant writes:

"Why historians have neglected to mention the part played by Philip Whitwell Wilson in Lenin's early revolutionary activities remains a mystery. That a soon-to-be-serving Member of Parliament played host to a suspected terrorist at the height of an ongoing revolution just has to be worthy of mention, but to date, it's escaped the attention of everyone."[309]

Historians are not the only ones who turned a blind eye to the Wilson-Lenin relationship. Even British police assigned to monitor Russian troublemakers in 1905 pointedly ignored the strange goings-on at 16 Percy Circus. Sarjeant writes:

"As Dr Robert Henderson points out in his 2020 book, *The Spark that Lit the Revolution*, Edgar Farce, the Okhrana's top agent who was working with Special Branch detectives in Hammersmith, failed to make any reference to Lenin's stay at 16 Percy Circus, despite the meticulousness he showed in logging and monitoring Lenin's colleagues at neighbouring addresses. Could this be an indication that Lenin was in London with the full cooperation of the British Secret Service? It's unlikely, but not impossible."

A careful researcher, Sarjeant refrains from jumping to any conclusion regarding the nature of Wilson's relationship with British intelligence. Nonetheless, in his meticulously-documented article, "Lenin at 16 Percy Circus, London," Sarjeant catalogs Wilson's extensive interactions with known intelligence networks, allowing us to draw our own conclusions.[310]

One of Wilson's closest friends, going back to 1903, at least, was Charles Masterman, whom Sarjeant describes as a "fellow radical Liberal...

who would eventually lead the War Propaganda Bureau at Wellington House…" As Britain's wartime propaganda chief during World War I, Masterman worked closely with Edwyn Bevan, the brother of Churchill's favorite conspiracy author Nesta Webster, whose works we have discussed extensively in the preceding pages. Masterman also worked closely with top-tier journalists such as Wickham Steed, editor of *The Times* of London; H.A. Gwynne, editor of the London *Morning Post*, and Robert Wilton, Petrograd correspondent for *The Times*; all of whom used their influential newspapers to promote the theory that the Bolsheviks were controlled by a cabal of "super-capitalist" Jews and Germans, as discussed in Chapter 28.

Masterman was closely involved with the core group of British insiders who groomed Lenin and other Bolshevik leaders in London. Sarjeant informs us that Wilson met Masterman through their mutual involvement with Toynbee Hall, a settlement house in East London. In fact, Toynbee Hall was the very first settlement house, established in 1884 by a small circle of Oxford Ruskinites, led by Alfred Milner. It became the prototype for a worldwide movement. A settlement house is "an organization by which educated, upper-class people could live in the slums in order to assist, instruct, and guide the poor, with particular emphasis on social welfare and adult education," as Carroll Quigley explains in his 1966 book *Tragedy and Hope*.[311]

Milner named Toynbee Hall after his closest friend and classmate Arnold Toynbee, a young Oxford historian who had delivered, with Milner, two lecture series in 1882, on the topic of Karl Marx, socialism, and the importance of both to the preservation of the British Empire, as discussed in Chapter 17. Tragically, Toynbee died the following year, in 1883, at the young age of 30. Milner insisted on naming the new settlement house after his lost friend.

It was not by chance, then, that Lenin found himself speaking at Toynbee Hall on June 17, 1902, during his first visit to London. It had become an icon of the Ruskinite movement. In keeping with Ruskin's principles, Toynbee Hall featured freewheeling debates where radicals and establishment figures could trade views as equals. In that spirit, Lenin engaged in a robust debate with Liberal MP John Morley on the topic of British foreign policy. Lenin asked him, "What is the use of your coming to the East End and talking about your foreign policy? Who there understands or cares about it?" Evidently, Lenin impressed his hosts. A few days later, he was invited back to Toynbee Hall for tea with Dean Robinson, who was both Toynbee Hall director and Dean of Oxford's Balliol House. Lenin lectured Robinson on the need for violent revolution, declaring, "The Imperialist British Empire will dissolve."[312]

Cecil Rhodes had died less than three months before, on March 26, 1902, leaving Milner in charge of his secret society. We do not know if Milner met with Lenin on his 1902 visit, but it does not seem out of the question, as Milner served on the governing board of Toynbee Hall, and was deeply involved in its affairs.

Whether or not the two met, their destinies were interlocked. As described in Chapter 18, Milner traveled to Petrograd in February, 1917, as War Secretary, delivering to Tsar Nicholas II a final ultimatum, on behalf of the British government. Two weeks later, the Tsar was overthrown, and the way cleared for Lenin's ascent to power.

CHAPTER 34

THE BALANCE OF POWER

O N FEBRUARY 23, 1945, Winston Churchill was dining at Chequers—
the country home of the Prime Minister—with two of his closest
advisors, Air Chief Marshall Sir Arthur Harris and Cabinet Secretary Sir
Edward Bridges. Churchill had just returned from the Yalta conference.
His thoughts were somber. Churchill was reportedly despondent because
his American counterpart Franklin Roosevelt had supposedly just given
away half of Europe to Stalin at the Yalta conference, an outcome that
Churchill was ostensibly helpless to prevent.

Churchill worried aloud what would happen once the Allies had finished bombing Germany into ruins. "What will lie between the white
snows of Russia and the white cliffs of Dover?" he asked. Would the
Russians stop? Would they sweep right through to the Atlantic? "There is
an unspoken fear in many people's hearts," said Churchill. "After this war,
we should be weak, we should have no money and no strength and we
should lie between the two great powers of the USA and the USSR."[313] The
next day, February 24, Churchill shared a similar thought with President
Beneš of Czechoslovakia and his Foreign Secretary Jan Masaryk. "A small

lion was walking between a huge Russian bear and a great American elephant, but perhaps it would prove to be the lion who knew the way," said Churchill.[314]

CHURCHILL'S PLAN

Churchill did indeed know the way. British statesmen had been following the same strategy for centuries. They called it the "balance of power." It was a strategy that enabled a small country like Britain to manipulate and outmaneuver larger countries. The key was to keep the larger countries fighting each other. In 1917, Sun Yat-sen, founder of the Chinese Republic, explained Britain's strategy in these words:

> "When England befriends another country, the purpose is not to maintain a cordial friendship for the sake of friendship but to utilize that country as a tool to fight a third country. When an enemy has been shorn of his power, he is turned into a friend, and the friend who has become strong, into an enemy. England always remains in a commanding position; she makes other countries fight her wars and she herself reaps the fruits of victory. She has been doing so for hundreds of years."[315]

This is what Churchill meant when he said, "perhaps it would prove to be the lion who knew the way." The English lion knew exactly what to do when caught between a "huge Russian bear" and a "great American elephant." You simply get them to fight each other. And you keep them fighting each other until their strength is spent. Thus was born the Cold War, in the mind of Winston Churchill, on February 24, 1945.

How Churchill Caused the Cold War

In fact, Churchill's despondency after the Yalta conference had little to do with Roosevelt allegedly giving away Eastern Europe. Four months before Yalta, Churchill had already handed over most of the Balkan countries to Stalin in an October 9, 1944 dinner meeting at the Kremlin, with no Americans present. Churchill drew up the so-called "Percentages Agreement" on a sheet of paper, listing the disputed countries and the percentages of each that would be controlled by Russia and Great Britain. The Eastern Question was paramount in Churchill's mind. He insisted upon 90-percent control of Greece, to ensure British naval dominance over the Eastern Mediterranean and the Suez Canal. Stalin accepted 90 percent control over Romania and 75 percent over Bulgaria, while Hungary and Yugoslavia were to be split 50/50 each.[316]

Contrary to myth, Churchill was not at all troubled about handing over Eastern Europe to Stalin. What troubled him was the United States, whose support against Russia remained uncertain, as the Americans were not yet locked into a permanent military alliance with Britain. In fact, it was not until 1949 that the US finally signed the NATO agreement.

Playing Off the US Against the USSR

One of the enduring mysteries of the Cold War is why British intelligence behaved so carelessly in its dealings with the Soviets. Time after time, high-level British officials—including intelligence officers—were recruited by Soviet intelligence and allowed to operate for years as double agents for the Russians, with little or no interference from British authorities.

The case of the Cambridge Five stands out, as none of the perpetrators were prosecuted, not even John Cairncross, who leaked atomic secrets to the Soviets.[317] Three members of the spy ring defected to Moscow

(Donald Maclean and Guy Burgess in 1953, and Kim Philby in 1963). Anthony Blunt and John Cairncross were both granted immunity from prosecution in 1964.[318] The Cambridge Five turned over such massive quantities of secret documents to the Soviets that the Russians suspected they were being hoodwinked and given bad information. The Soviets were especially wary of Kim Philby, unable to comprehend how a person of known Communist sympathies and extensive involvement with Communist front groups could have risen to become a high-ranking officer of Britain's Secret Intelligence Service (SIS).[319]

The ease with which Soviet intelligence operated among British elites during the Cold War is usually ascribed to British incompetence and apathy. A more plausible explanation is that the British simply had a different relationship with the Soviets than we Americans did. British spymasters appear to have deliberately allowed their people to cooperate with the Soviets, behind the Americans' backs. By this means, they were able to play off Americans against Russians and Russians against Americans, in an endless game of "balance of power" that continues to this day.

CHAPTER 35

KISSINGER AND THE ROUND TABLE

H ENRY KISSINGER PLAYED a significant role in helping execute Churchill's plan to play off the Americans against the Communists. Kissinger had been well-trained for this role by his Harvard mentor William Yandell Elliott (1896-1979), an American historian and political scientist who was one of the early leaders of the Round Table Movement. "Whatever I have achieved, I owe importantly to his inspiration," Kissinger later wrote of Elliott.[320]

In his 2012 book *New World Order: A Strategy of Imperialism*, Sean Stone reveals the surprising extent of Elliott's influence on Kissinger. As an Oxford graduate and one of the original US Round Table members, Elliott acted, for decades, as an agent of British influence in Washington. He was a behind-the-scenes kingmaker who advised six US presidents. Around 1951, Elliott recruited Kissinger into the newly-formed CIA.[321] However, both men cultivated relationships with the British government that arguably conflicted with their loyalties as US intelligence officers.

British Agent of Influence

Elliot's connection with the British establishment dated back to 1919-1923, when he earned his doctorate at Balliol College, Oxford. There he was recruited into Milner's Round Table Group. "[M]embers of the Round Table practically ran the college in the early 20th century," notes Stone. Elliott's Oxford mentor, Alexander Dunlop Lindsay, was a close friend of Round Table founder Alfred Milner.[322] Through his work with the Round Table, Elliott developed close ties with British intelligence, going so far as to engage, in the run-up to World War II, in British operations targeting US citizens deemed to be opponents of the war.[323]

At Harvard, Elliott taught Kissinger to see the world through British eyes. Many things about America displeased the Round Tablers. What they found most infuriating was America's independence, its ability to do as it liked, without regard for the wishes of foreign powers. The Round Tablers had never forgiven the US Senate for rejecting the League of Nations. Woodrow Wilson had promised the Round Table he would join the League, but the US Senate had overruled him. Clearly the Senate had too much power, the Round Tablers concluded. Elliott dutifully sought to remedy this problem. In 1935, he wrote an influential book called *The Need for Constitutional Reform* calling for an all-powerful US presidency able to make treaties without Senate approval.[324]

Breaking American Pride

Under Elliott's tutelage, Kissinger learned to put British interests ahead of America's. This was the heart and soul of the Round Table agenda, and Kissinger learned it well. He devoted his life to breaking US power, so we would have to accept British plans for global government. Kissinger was fated to be the hammer that would break America's pride.

On May 10, 1982, Kissinger spoke at the Royal Institute of International Affairs (RIIA) in London, known as Chatham House. He was on home ground at the RIIA, an institution founded by Milner's Round Table and wholly devoted to its goals. Knowing he was among friends, Kissinger spoke with unusual candor about the special relationship between the US and UK, and about the peculiar role Kissinger had played personally in promoting British interests in Washington. Referring to the period during and after World War II, Kissinger said:

> "The British were so matter-of-factly helpful that they became a participant in internal American deliberations, to a degree probably never before practiced between sovereign nations. ... In my White House incarnation then, I kept the British Foreign Office better informed and more closely engaged than I did the American State Department."[325]

The period of what Kissinger called his "White House incarnation" would have been 1973-1977, when he served as National Security Advisor (1969-1975) and Secretary of State (1973-1977) for Presidents Nixon and Ford. These were years of unprecedented crisis for America, including defeat in Vietnam and Nixon's forced resignation. Kissinger's admission that he "kept the British Foreign Office better informed and more closely engaged" than his own State Department during these perilous years raises questions of motive, loyalty, and judgment. It could be argued that Kissinger's 1982 speech constitutes an admission that he was, in fact, acting as a double agent for the British.

LOSING VIETNAM ON PURPOSE

For most Americans, defeat in Vietnam was a bitter and senseless tragedy. Kissinger, however, seemed to view it in a positive light, as a necessary course correction for America. When Kissinger spoke of America's "rude awakening" in his 1982 speech at Chatham House, he could hardly conceal a tone of grim satisfaction. Kissinger said:

> "It was therefore a rude awakening when in the 1960s and 70s the United States became conscious of the limits of even *its* resources. Now with a little over a fifth of the world's GNP, America was powerful but no longer dominant. Vietnam was the trauma and the catharsis but the recognition was bound to come in any event. Starting in the 70s, for the first time, the United States has had to conduct a foreign policy in the sense with which Europeans have always been familiar: as one country among many, unable either to dominate the world or escape from it, with the necessity of accommodation, maneuver, a sensitivity to marginal shifts in the balance of power, an awareness of continuity and of the interconnections between events."[326]

Of course, defeat in Vietnam had not come out of the blue. It was a man-made catastrophe, not a natural phenomenon like the weather. Kissinger himself had been largely responsible for the disaster. Moreover, while Kissinger was negotiating "peace" with the North Vietnamese, he was, by his own admission, keeping the British Foreign Office "better informed and more closely engaged" than his own State Department. Kissinger's statement raises questions about the role of Great Britain in the Vietnam debacle.

As Kissinger tells it—and as his audience at Chatham House would have fully understood—the Vietnam War achieved one of the core objectives of Milner's Round Table. It humbled America, teaching her to accept her place as one nation among many in the global "commonwealth." In his zeal to attain this goal, Kissinger may have leaned on the scales a bit, deliberately "allowing the war in Vietnam to drag on … " according to Stone.[327] It was, in fact, the prolonged nature of the war that finally turned public opinion against it. US forces were engaged in Vietnam for 20 years, from 1955-1975, with massive ground forces deployed from 1965-1973, leaving more than 58,000 Americans dead. Something had to break eventually.

NOT HUMBLE ENOUGH YET?

While applauding the chastening effects of the Vietnam War in his 1982 speech, Kissinger made clear that the US had a long way to go before completing its lesson in humility. "[I]t will be a slow, painful, perhaps bitter process," said Kissinger. His words proved prophetic. The humbling process continues to this day. It may or may not be coincidental that the man currently in charge of administering this bitter pill to America happens to be yet another Round Table disciple, Klaus Schwab, founder and executive chairman of the World Economic Forum.

CHAPTER 36

FROM ROUND TABLE TO WEF

I N A MARCH 10, 2022 article, UK journalist Johnny Vedmore revealed that Klaus Schwab's mentor at Harvard University was none other than Henry Kissinger. Schwab studied at Harvard's John F. Kennedy School of Government in the 1966-1967 academic year. There Kissinger recruited him into a CIA-funded program called the Harvard International Summer Seminar, directed by Kissinger. In the process, says Vedmore, Kissinger also recruited Schwab into the Round Table network. [328]

The Harvard International Summer Seminar was, in fact, founded by William Yandell Elliott and his then-graduate student Kissinger in 1951, for the express purpose of recruiting and training promising young people to be apostles for the Round Table agenda. [329] Vedmore notes that, "Elliott, along with many of his star pupils," served as "the key connectors between the American national security establishment and the British 'Round Table' movement, embodied by organisations such as Chatham House in the UK and the Council on Foreign Relations in the United States." [330] Although Milner's Round Table technically no longer existed by the 1950s—at least not under that name—Vedmore correctly notes that the network lived on through the institutions it created, especially Chatham House and the Council on Foreign Relations.

Thanks to Stone and Vedmore, we now see that Alfred Milner mentored A. D. Lindsay; Lindsay mentored William Yandell Elliott; Elliott mentored Henry Kissinger; and Kissinger mentored Klaus Schwab. By linking Kissinger to Schwab, Vedmore has proved that a direct line of descent connects Schwab to Alfred Milner, founder of the Round Table Movement. Not surprisingly, Schwab and his World Economic Forum continue pushing the Round Table's perennial agenda of humbling America, this time under the banner of "multipolarism," which seeks to replace an ostensibly US-dominated world order with a new system revolving around the so-called BRICS states, among whom Russia, China, Brazil, India, and South Africa are supposedly paramount.

It lies beyond the scope of this book to explore Klaus Schwab's agenda and the many ways in which it perpetuates and extends the Round Table program. Suffice it to say that the extraordinary power and status that has mysteriously accrued to the World Economic Forum in recent years is difficult to explain without taking into the account the hidden power of the Round Table network.

For Americans, the situation has changed little since June 15, 1919, that sorrowful day when the last US troops withdrew from the Russian Civil War, as described in Chapter 21. "[N]ot a soldier knew, not even vaguely, why he had fought or why he was going now, and why his comrades were left behind—so many of them beneath the wooden crosses," remarked Lieutenant John Cudahy of the US 339th regiment at the time.[331] So it remains, to this day, on countless battlefields across the world, as America struggles and bleeds to create a New World Order that we never wanted, never understood, and that was never our idea in the first place.

CHAPTER 37

CHURCHILL'S GHOST

A LL OVER BRITAIN today, statues of Winston Churchill are being van-
dalized and defaced. He is called a "racist," an "imperialist," an
"anti-Semite," and a "white supremacist." I do not wish to add my voice to
that unseemly chorus. There are few men in history I admire more than
Churchill. I forgive him his faults. Nonetheless, this historical correction
must be made.

THE COURAGE TO BE WRONG

When a 23-year-old Churchill rode in one of the last great cavalry charges
in British history, at Omdurman in 1898, he showed physical courage of
a sort our present age has forgotten.[332] When he took up his pen in 1920
to write that article for the *Illustrated Sunday Herald*, Churchill showed a
different sort of courage, which our age has also forgotten. He showed the
courage to speak plainly, even when he was wrong.

Nothing is deeper or darker than an ethnic grudge, and no hatred
blacker than the enmity between Slav and Jew which has stained the
steppe lands red for a thousand years. It takes courage to wade into someone else's blood feud, and courage to speak one's mind bluntly. Churchill

showed such courage, even where he got the story wrong. We must commend him for that.

Because Churchill had the courage to speak his mind, we too may speak, a hundred years later. We may ask questions we never dared ask, and perhaps obtain answers we did not expect. A hundred years of lies have buried many truths about the world's first Communist state. It will take more than this book to restore those truths to light. But if these words inspire even a few curious souls to dig deeper, I am content.

ENDNOTES

1   Winston Churchill, "Zionism versus Bolshevism," *Illustrated Sunday Herald*, February 8, 1920, page 5: https://archive.org/details/WinstonChurchillZionismVsBolshevismStruggleForTheSoulOfTheJewishPeople1920

2   "Russian Civil War," *Encyclopedia Britannica*/Britannica.com, Last updated November 27, 2022; Werth Nicolas, "Crimes and Mass Violence of the Russian Civil Wars (1918-1921)," SciencesPo.fr, March 21, 2008: https://www.sciencespo.fr/mass-violence-war-massacre-resistance/en/document/crimes-and-mass-violence-russian-civil-wars-1918-1921.html

3   "Parliamentary Paper, *Russia. No. 1: A Collection of Reports on Bolshevism in Russia*, Great Britain, Foreign Office (London: His Majesty's Stationery Office, April 1919)

4   Alan Sarjeant, *The Protocols Matrix: George Shanks and the Protocols of the Elders of Zion* (2021), page 21: https://www.academia.edu/51197716/George_Shanks_the_Protocols_of_the_Elders_of_Zion_and_the_Committee_on_Russian_Affairs

5   Sarjeant, *The Protocols Matrix* (2021), abstract

6   Sarjeant, *The Protocols Matrix* (2021): "George Shanks, the man who published the first English translation of *The Protocols of the Elders of*

Zion in January 1920 was working as a clerk in the Chief Whip's Office at 12 Downing Street under Coalition Whip, Freddie Guest. A closer look at Shanks' background also reveals he was the nephew of Aylmer Maude, the famous friend and translator of Tolstoy who became a leading voice in the pro-Interventionist movement of the Russian Affairs Committee during the Russian Civil War of 1917 to 1922. Maude's colleagues at this time included former members of Britain's wartime propaganda bureau in Petrograd, Harold Williams, Bernard Pares and Hugh Walpole … A brand new find also reveals that Shanks co-translator, Major Edward G.G. Burdon was serving as Secretary to the United Russia Societies Association under House of Commons Speaker, James Lowther and alongside members Sir Bernard Pares, John Buchan and Hugh Walpole in support of White Russia's war against the Bolsheviks … " (abstract); "[Robert Hobart] Cust went on to reveal that Shanks, who had served in both the Royal Navy Air Service and the Anglo-Russia supplies committee during the war, had been assisted in the translation by Edward Griffiths George Burdon OBE, a decorated Temporary Major previously attached to the 4th Northumberland Fusiliers." (page 159)

7　Sarjeant, *The Protocols Matrix* (2021): "Shanks is alleged to have solicited an original Russian copy of the book from the British Museum in autumn of 1919, carried out a translation and then approached the highly respectable government printers, Eyre & Spottiswoode Ltd with an order to produce a staggering 30,000 copies of the book at his own expense (by contrast only 20,000 copies of F. Scott Fitzgerald's *The Great Gatsby* were pressed by Charles Scribner's Sons during its initial run in June 1925)." (page 20); "Robert Hobart Cust was a friend of Major Edward Griffiths

Burdon OBE, the man who had helped George Shanks translate The Protocols from Russia into English. Cust claims to have introduced Shanks to Eyre & Spottiswoode, 'His Majesty's' printers." (page 177): "The choice of Eyre & Spottiswoode may well have been a reflection of the proximity of the Cust family to His Majesty, Edward VII. Robert's cousin was Lionel Cust, son of Sir Reginald Cust, who had served not only as Director of the National Portrait Gallery but also as 'Gentleman Usher' to the King and Surveyor of the King's Pictures. Eyre & Spottiswoode was 'His Majesty's' printers, and attached to the Stationery Office of the British Government (the HMSO). Since 1901, the company would have handled practically anything relating to public information including government white papers and the various Gazettes. In any other circumstances, the link between The Protocols and the King's Printers would be a fairly casual connection, but the Cust family's reputation and status in the Royal household would certainly account for the clinching of a deal with such a highly regarded printing house from such unproven authors." (page 261)

8   Sarjeant, *The Protocols Matrix* (2021), page 20

9   Sarjeant, *The Protocols Matrix* (2021), page 20

10 Advertisement, *Evening Standard* (London), July 20, 1920, page 11

11 "'The Jewish Peril': A Disturbing Pamphlet: Call for Inquiry," *The Times* (London), May 8, 1920, page 15: "What are these 'Protocols'? Are they authentic? If so, what malevolent assembly concocted these plans, and gloated over their exposition? Are they a forgery? If so, whence comes the uncanny note of prophecy, prophecy in parts fulfilled, in parts far gone in the way of fulfillment? Have we been struggling these tragic years to blow up and extirpate the secret

organization of German world dominion only to find beneath it another more dangerous because more secret? Have we, by straining every fibre of our national body, escaped a 'Pax Germanica' only to fall into a 'Pax Judaica'? The 'Elders of Zion,' as represented in their 'Protocols' are by no means kinder taskmasters than William II. and his henchmen would have been."

12   Richard Pipes: "Solzhenitsyn and the Jews, revisited: Alone Together," *The New Republic*, November 25, 2002; Richard Pipes, "Solzhenitsyn's Troubled Prophetic Mission," *The Moscow Times*, August 7, 2008; "Parliamentary Paper, *Russia. No. 1: A Collection of Reports on Bolshevism in Russia*, Great Britain, Foreign Office (London: His Majesty's Stationery Office, April 1919)

13   Richard Norton Taylor, "MI5 detained Trotsky on way to revolution: Public records: Russian was arrested on British orders in 1917 on a boat in Canada but released after intervention by MI6," *The Guardian*, July 5, 2001: "Leon Trotsky, the creator of the Red Army, was detained on the orders of MI5 ...Trotsky was arrested with five Russian comrades. There he could have remained, had it not been for the intervention of the Secret Intelligence Service, MI6. Claude Dansey, an MI6 officer, had also just landed at Halifax. ... Dansey reported: 'I told Wiseman he had better be discharged at once, and he said that he was going to do so.' Within four weeks of his arrest, to MI5's chagrin, Trotsky and his fellow revolutionaries boarded another ship heading for Russia."; George Buchanan, *My Mission to Russia, Volume II* (London, New York, Toronto and Melbourne: Cassell and Company, Ltd, 1923), pp 120-121: In his memoirs, George Buchanan claims that it was he who gave the order to release Trotsky, and that he did it to appease British socialists and the Labour Party. "I

am anxious to conciliate the Labour party and the Socialists ... I then reminded him [Foreign Minister Miliukoff] that I had, early in April, informed him that Trotzky and other Russian political refugees were being detained at Halifax until the wishes of the Provisional Government with regard to them had been ascertained. On April 8 I had, at his request, asked my Government to release them and to allow them to proceed on their journey to Russia." Richard B. Spence, "Interrupted Journey: British Intelligence and the Arrest of Leon Trotskii, April 1917," *Revolutionary Russia*, Volume 13, No. 1, June 1, 2000, pp 1-28; [From abstract] "Among its findings is that Trotskii's arrest was the work of one branch of British intelligence, but his return to Russia was facilitated by another. Circumstantial evidence suggests that the same agency [MI6] sought to recruit or manipulate Trotskii as an agent of influence in revolutionary Russia." Robert Service, *Trotsky: A Biography* (Cambridge, Massachusetts: The Belknap Press/Harvard University Press, 2009), page 159; Richard B. Spence, "Hidden Agendas: Spies, Lies and Intrigue Surrounding Trotsky's American Visit of January-April 1917," *Revolutionary Russia*, Volume 21, Issue 1, 2008, pages 33-55: [From abstract] "Trotsky was surrounded by a web of intrigue and agents of various stripes throughout, and even before, his American stay. He became a pawn, knowingly or not, in assorted plots. Trotsky was the target of a scheme by elements of the British intelligence services to secure his cooperation in revolutionary Russia."

14   Keith Jeffery, *MI6: The History of the Secret Intelligence Service 1909-1949* (London: Bloomsbury, 2010); Antony Sutton, *Wall Street and the Bolshevik Revolution* (West Hoathly, UK: Clairview Books, 2012), page 25

15   Anita Leslie, *Cousin Clare: The Tempestuous Career of Clare Sheridan* (London: Hutchinson & Co., 1976) pp 116-126; Robert Service, *Trotsky: A Biography* (Cambridge, Massachusetts: The Belknap Press/ Harvard University Press, 2009), pp 264-266

16   P.J. Capelotti, *Our Man in the Crimea: Commander Hugo Koehler and the Russian Civil War* (Columbia, SC: University of South Carolina, 1991), pp 173-174

17   Norman B. Deuel, "Claims Trotsky was British Spy," United Press International, March 5, 1938

18   "In the years 1902 to 1903, [Phillip Whitwell] Wilson had lived at Toynbee Hall... Wilson's knowledge of Lenin and Trotsky clearly dated back to this period... Lenin himself had spoken at Toynbee Hall during his first visit to London in 1902. (...) Wilson's passing encounters with Trotsky at Toynbee would take on an additional resonance after his move to New York... In a curious twist, Wilson would end-up living just several hundred yards from... Louis C. Fraina... the man who perhaps did more than anybody to help Trotsky settle-in in New York during his three-month stay in the Bronx between January and March 1917. (...) It's entirely possible that Wilson's arrival in New York in the first week of January 1918 was linked in some way to the work of the Propaganda Bureau ... " Alan Sarjeant, "Lenin at 16 Percy Circus, London," pixelsurgery. wordpress.com, November 30, 2011: https://pixelsurgery. wordpress.com/2011/11/30/percy-circus-london [accessed April 17, 2024]

19   George Buchanan, *My Mission to Russia, Volume II* (London, New York, Toronto and Melbourne: Cassell and Company, Ltd, 1923), pp

92-106, 140; cited in Dr. Stanley Monteith, *Brotherhood of Darkness* (Oklahoma City, OK: Hearthstone Publishing, 2000), page 36

20   Princess Paley, "Mes Souvenirs de Russie," *Revue de Paris*, June 1, 1922

21   Princess Paley, *Memories of Russia 1916-1919* (London, Herbert Jenkins Limited, 1924), page 42

22   Maurice Paléologue (Last French Ambassador to the Russian Court), *An Ambassador's Memoirs, Volume III* (August 19, 1916-May 17, 1917), translated by F.A. Holt, O.B.E. (London: Hutchinson & Co. Ltd, 1925), pp 129-130

23   Andrew Cook, *To Kill Rasputin: The Life and Death of Grigori Rasputin* (Stroud, Gloucestershire, UK; The History Press, 2006), pp 213-221; George Buchanan, *My Mission to Russia, Volume II* (London, New York, Toronto and Melbourne: Cassell and Company, Ltd, 1923), page 51: " … having heard that His Majesty suspected a young Englishman, who had been a college friend of Prince Felix Yusupoff, of having been concerned in Rasputin's murder, I took the opportunity of assuring him that the suspicion was absolutely groundless. His Majesty thanked me and said that he was very glad to hear this."

24   *The Great War: The Standard History of the All-Europe Conflict, Vol. 9,* editors H.W. Wilson, J.A. Hammerton (London, The Amalgamated Press Ltd, 1917), page 117

25   Princess Paley, *Memories of Russia 1916-1919* (London, Herbert Jenkins Limited, 1924), pp 295-300, 313

26   Princess Paley (1924), pp 41-42

27   Lancelot L. Farrar, Jr., *Divide and Conquer. German Efforts to Conclude*

a Separate Peace, 1914-1918 (Boulder, Colorado, *East European Quarterly*, 1978), page 18

28   "Constantinople Agreement," *Encyclopedia Britannica*/Britannica. com, Last updated November 27, 2022: The secret Constantinople Agreement between France, Britain and Russia was worked out in a series of diplomatic communications from March 4 to April 10, 1915. Opinions vary as to the date when the Agreement actually became operative. The *Encyclopedia Britannica* gives the date of the treaty as March 18, 1915, which corresponds to the date of telegram No. 1226, sent by Russian Foreign Minister Sergey Sazonov to Alexander Izvolsky, the Russian Ambassador to Paris, stating, "Now the British Government has given its complete consent in writing to the annexation by Russia of the Straits and Constantinople within the limits indicated by us, and only demanded security for its economic interests and a similar benevolent attitude on our part towards the political aspirations of England in other parts." The text of this telegram appears in F. Seymour Cocks, *The Secret Treaties and Understandings* (London: Union of Democratic Control, 1918), pp 17-18. It should be noted that Cocks's *The Secret Treaties and Understandings* gives the date of the Constantinople Agreement as March 20, 1915 (see page 15). Also on page 15, the substance of the treaty is summarized thus: "Britain consents to the annexation by Russia of the Straits and Constantinople, in return for a similar benevolent attitude on Russia's part towards the political aspirations of Britain in other parts. The neutral zone in Persia to be included in the British sphere of influence. The districts adjoining Ispahan and Yezd to be included in Russian sphere, in which Russia is to be granted 'full liberty of action.'"

29   Princess Paley (1924), pp 41-42

30   David Fromkin, *A Peace to End All Peace: The Fall of the Ottoman Empire and the Creation of the Modern Middle East* (New York: Henry Holt & Company LLC, 1989), page 98: "In Kitchener's view, Germany was an enemy in Europe and Russia was an enemy in Asia: the paradox of the 1914 war in which Britain and Russia were allied was that by winning in Europe, Britain risked losing in Asia. The only completely satisfactory outcome of the war, from Kitchener's point of view, was for Germany to lose it without Russia winning it—and in 1914 it was not clear how that could be accomplished. So the War Minister planned to strike first in the coming postwar struggle with Russia for control of the road to and into India."

31   Malcolm Yapp, "The Legend of the Great Game," *Proceedings of the British Academy: 2000 Lectures and Memoirs*, vol. 111, May 16, 2000), Oxford University Press, pp. 179–198; Seymour Becker, "The 'Great Game': The History of an Evocative Phrase." *Asian Affairs* 43.1 (2012): 61-80

32   "The Muscovy Company: World's first joint stock company,"tbsnews. net, July 25, 2021: https://www.tbsnews.net/features/panorama/muscovy-company-worlds-first-joint-stock-company-278674

33   Jeremy Black, *British Foreign Policy in an Age of Revolutions, 1783-1793* (Cambridge, UK: Cambridge University Press, 1994). p. 290; John Ehrman, *The Younger Pitt, Volume II: The Reluctant Transition* (Stanford, CA: Stanford University Press, 1996) pp xx.

34   The British "balance of power" doctrine—which Britain still uses today—was explained by Sun Yat-sen in his 1917 book *The Vital Problem of China*. He wrote: "The key policy of England is to attack the strongest country with the help of weaker countries, and join

the weakened enemy in checking the growth of a third country. The British foreign policy has remained basically unchanged for two centuries. When England befriends another country, the purpose is not to maintain a cordial friendship for the sake of friendship but to utilize that country as a tool to fight a third country. When an enemy has been shorn of his power, he is turned into a friend, and the friend who has become strong, into an enemy. England always remains in a commanding position; she makes other countries fight her wars and she herself reaps the fruits of victory. She has been doing so for hundreds of years." Sun Yat-sen, *The Vital Problem of China* (Taipei, Taiwan: China Cultural Service, 1953), page 78

35   Christine Hatt, *Catherine the Great* (London: Evans Brothers, Ltd, 2002) pp 32, 35, 59

36   Bernard Pares, *A History of Russia* (New York: Alfred A. Knopf, 1926), pp 28-30, 87-98

37   Jeremy Black, *British Foreign Policy in an Age of Revolutions, 1783-1793* (Cambridge, UK: Cambridge University Press, 1994). p. 290; John Ehrman, *The Younger Pitt, Volume II: The Reluctant Transition* (Stanford, CA: Stanford University Press, 1996) pp xx.

38   George Finlay, LL.D., *History of the Greek Revolution, Volume I* (Edinburgh and London: William Blackwood and Sons, 1861), pp 68, 121, 123, 164-168, 189-191, 239-240

39   Edward Hertslet (1875). "General treaty between Great Britain, Austria, France, Prussia, Russia, Sardinia and Turkey, signed at Paris on 30th March 1856: The Map of Europe by Treaty showing the various political and territorial changes which have taken place since the general peace of 1814, with numerous maps and notes." Vol. 2. London: Butterworth. pp. 1250–1265.

40   David Fromkin, *A Peace to End All Peace: The Fall of the Ottoman Empire and the Creation of the Modern Middle East* (New York: Henry Holt & Company LLC, 1989), page 27: "Defeating Russian designs in Asia emerged as the obsessive goal of generations of British civilian and military officials. Their attempt to do so was, for them, 'the Great Game,' in which the stakes ran high. George Curzon, the future Viceroy of India, defined the stakes clearly: 'Turkestan, Afghanistan, Transcaspia, Persia... they are the pieces on a chessboard upon which is being played out a game for the *dominion of the world.*' Queen Victoria put it even more clearly: it was, she said, 'a question of Russian or British supremacy in the world.'"

41   George Earle Buckle, *The Life of Benjamin Disraeli Earl of Beaconsfield, Volume VI, 1876-1881* (London: John Murray, Albemarle Street, W., 1920), page 148; cited in Edward E. Slosson, "The Unveiling of Victoria," *The Independent*, November 6, 1920, pp 189-190

42   Buckle (1920), pp 189-190

43   Buckle (1920), pp 189-190

44   Buckle (1920), pp 189-190

45   Buckle (1920), pp 189-190

46   Viscount Stratford de Redcliffe, *The Eastern Question* (London: John Murray, 1881) page xix

47   L.L. Farrar, Jr., *Divide and Conquer. German Efforts to Conclude a Separate Peace, 1914-1918*, (1978), pp. 13-56; Stevenson, David: *The First World War and International Politics*, New York 1988, pp. 92-95; Fischer, Fritz, Germany's Aims in the First World War, New York 1961, pp 184f, 189

48   Sir George Buchanan to Sir Edward Grey 1/1/15; in Winston S. Churchill, vol. 3, Companion, Part I, Documents, July 1914—April

1915, ed. Martin Gilbert (London: Heinemann, 1972), pp 359–60; cited in Prior, Robin. *Gallipoli: The End of the Myth* (p. 253). Yale University Press. Kindle Edition.

49   Harvey Broadbent, "Gallipoli: One Great Deception?" Australian Broadcasting Corporation, April 23, 2009: https://www.abc.net.au/news/2009-04-24/30630

50   Broadbent, "Gallipoli: One Great Deception?" ABC, April 23, 2009

51   Lancelot L. Farrar, Jr., *Divide and Conquer. German Efforts to Conclude a Separate Peace, 1914-1918* (Boulder, Colorado, East European Quarterly, 1978), page 18

52   *Proceedings of the Brest-Litovsk Peace Conference*, 21 November, 1917-3 March, 1918 (Washington DC: Government Printing Office, 1918), page 49; Louis Fischer, *Oil Imperialism: The International Struggle for Petroleum* (New York: International Publishers, 1926), pp 212-214

53   "Attack on the Kremlin," *The Times* (London), November 19, 1917, page 8

54   F. Seymour Cocks, *The Secret Treaties and Understandings* (London: Union of Democratic Control, 1918), pp 12

55   "Lenin's Peace Decree Ready for Issue," *The Times* (London), November 26, 1917, page 8

56   "Statement by Trotsky on the Publication of the Secret Treaties," November 22, 1917, reprinted in *Soviet Documents on Foreign Policy, Vol. 1 (1917–1924)*, edited by Jane Degras (New York: Oxford University Press, 1951), p31

57   Cocks, *The Secret Treaties and Understandings* (1918), page 25

58   *Proceedings of the Brest-Litovsk Peace Conference*, November 21, 1917 – March 3, 1918 (Washington DC: Government Printing Office, 1918), page 49; Louis Fischer, *Oil Imperialism: The International*

Struggle for Petroleum (New York: International Publishers, 1926), pp 212-214

59 Anglo-Persian Oil Company (Acquisition of Capital) HC Deb 07 July 1914vol64cc1032-55:https://api.parliament.uk/historic-hansard/commons/1914/jul/07/anglo-persian-oil-company-acquisition-of-1

60 A. R. Begli Beigie, "Repeating mistakes: Britain, Iran & the 1919 Treaty," *The Iranian*, March 27, 2001; https://iranian.com/History/2001/March/Britain/index.html

61 Louis Fischer, *Oil Imperialism: The International Struggle for Petroleum* (New York: International Publishers, 1926), page 218

62 David Horowitz and Richard Poe, *The Shadow Party: How George Soros, Hillary Clinton, and Sixties Radicals Seized Control of the Democratic Party* (Nashville, TN: Thomas Nelson, 2006), pp 231-243

63 In *The Shadow Party*, the two examples we gave of collaborating front groups were the Albert Einstein Institution and the International Center on Strategic Non-Violence. I have since learned that the National Endowment for Democracy (US) and the Westminster Foundation for Democracy (UK) are more important nodes in this network, and therefore better examples. Horowitz and Poe, *The Shadow Party* (2006), pp 232-233

64 Horowitz and Poe, *The Shadow Party* (2006), pp 232-233

65 Marcie Smith, "Getting Gene Sharp Wrong," jacobin.com, December 2, 2019; See also, Marcie Smith, "Change Agent: Gene Sharp's Neoliberal Nonviolence (Part One)," nonsite.org, May 10, 2019

66 Ruaridh Arrow, *Gene Sharp: How to Start a Revolution* (Big Indy Limited, 2020), pp 67-71

67 Horowitz and Poe, *The Shadow Party* (2006), page 233

68 Winston Churchill, "Zionism versus Bolshevism," *Illustrated Sunday Herald*, February 8, 1920, page 5: https://archive.org/details/WinstonChurchillZionismVsBolshevismStruggleForTheSoulOfTheJewishPeople1920

69 Micah Alpaugh, "The British Origins of the French Jacobins: Radical Sociability and the Development of Political Club Networks, 1787-1793," October 2014, *European History Quarterly*, Volume 44, No, 4, pp 593-619

70 Thomas Jefferson to Lafayette, founders.archives.gov, 14 February 1815

71 Thomas Jefferson to William Plumer, founders.archives.gov, 31 January 1815

72 Alpaugh, (October 2014), pp 593-619

73 Alpaugh (October 2014), pp 593-619

74 Alpaugh (October 2014), pp 594-596

75 Alpaugh (October 2014), pp 594-595

76 "News of a political act—the king's dismissal of his reformist Finance Minister Necker—had fired the original unrest in Paris. Nine days after the Bastille fell the Paris mob hung Necker's successor, and political authority was restored by the Marquis de Lafayette. He arrived on a white horse—literally as well as symbolically—and took military command of Paris on July 15 [1789] …Yet this seeming guarantor of continuing order amidst revolutionary change was soon denounced not just by the Right, but by the Left as well. Burke's conservative attack on the French Revolution listed 'Fayettism' first among the 'rabble of systems.' On the revolutionary side, 'Gracchus' Babeuf, just a year after the fall of the Bastille, excoriated Lafayette as

a conceited and antidemocratic brake on the revolutionary process. Later revolutionaries, as we shall see, repeatedly raged against him. ... (page 21) ... Lafayette ... was soon drowned out by the more bellicose and radical Brissot. The Brissotists, or Girondists, were in turn swept aside by the more extreme Jacobins in the late spring of 1793. The relatively moderate Jacobinism of Danton was then supplanted by Robespierre; his reign of terror claimed some forty thousand domestic victims in 1793-94. ... (page 22) ... The new republican Constitution of 1795 was far less radical than that written in 1793 (but never put in effect). Two years later the attempt of the Babeuf conspiracy to organize a new revolutionary uprising was crushed by the five-man Directory with no difficulty. (pp 22-23) ... The revolutionary egalitarianism of Babeuf, Marechal, and Restif de la Bretonne is the progenitor of modern Communism—and of revolutionary socialism, the rival ideal of revolutionary nationalism (page 71) ... .Babeuf was arrested and the conspiracy destroyed on May 10, 1796. (page 77): James H. Billington, *Fire in the Minds of Men: Origins of the Revolutionary Faith* (New York: Basic Books, 1980), pp 21-23, 72-78

77 "A generation later, Karl Marx and Friedrich Engels built on Buonarrotti's heroic narrative by naming Babeuf the first modern communist." Laura Mason, *The Last Revolutionaries: The Conspiracy Trial of Gracchus Babeuf and the Equals* (New Haven: Yale University Press, 2022), page 4

78 "Babeuf repeatedly used the word *communauté* (and inventions like *communautistes*) in the revolutionary manner of Restif." Billington, *Fire in the Minds of Men* (1980), page 83

79 "In 1785, Restif published a review of a book describing a

communal experiment in Marseilles. He cited a letter of 1782 from the book's author [Joseph-Alexandre-Victor Hupay de Fuve] who described himself as an *auteur communiste*—the first known appearance in print of this word. ... In February 1793, Restif used the term communism as his own for the first time to describe the fundamental change in ownership that would obviate the need for any further redistribution of goods and property. His detailed exposition of communism (and regular use of the word) began the following year with a 'Regulation ... for the establishment of a general Community of the Human Race' in his *Monsieur Nicolas or the human heart unveiled*. ... Restif's three-volume *Philosophie de Monsieur Nicolas* of 1796 called for a *communauté universelle*, and talked about "the Communists" as if they were active and numerous in the real world. The question of whether Restif was alluding to, or in some way connected with, Babeuf's concurrent conspiracy takes us deeper into the occult labyrinths of Paris where modern revolutionary organization began." Billington, *Fire in the Minds of Men* (1980), pp 79-85

80   "While no public suggestion of a link between Babeuf and Restif was raised at the former's public trial, the authorities, as they prepared their case, apparently believed that such a link existed ... A more serious link almost certainly lies in Maréchal, the journalistic protector and sponsor of Babeuf's early career who knew Restif well before the revolution and before meeting Babeuf. Maréchal's still obscure role in the conspiracy-like Restif, he escaped prosecution altogether despite his direct involvement-leads back in turn to the links that Babeuf, Restif, and Marechal all had with Bonneville's Social Circle." Billington, *Fire in the Minds of Men*, page 83

81   "The term 'communism' in the France of the 1840s denoted...
     an offshoot of the Jacobin tradition of the first French revolution,"
     wrote Marxist historian David Fernbach in 1973. "This communism
     went back to Gracchus Babeuf's Conspiracy of Equals... This
     egalitarian or 'crude' communism, as Marx called it originated
     before the great development of machine industry. It appealed to
     the Paris sans-culottes—artisans, journeymen and unemployed—
     and potentially to the poor peasantry in the countryside." David
     Fernbach, "Introduction" to *Karl Marx, The Revolutions of 1848* (New
     York: Random House, 1973), pp 17-18

82   Fernbach (1973), pp 17-18

83   *Augsburger Allgemeine Zeitung*, March 11, 1840, cited in Billington,
     Fire in the Minds of Men, page 246, 583

84   Billington, *Fire in the Minds of Men*, pp 71-72, 530

85   Billington, *Fire in the Minds of Men*, pp 72-73

86   Hélène Maspero Clerc, "Samuel Swinton, éditeur du Courier de
     l'Europe à Boulogne-sur-Mer (1778–1783) et agent secret du
     Gouvernement britannique", *Annales de la Révolution française*, no.
     266, oct–déc. 1985, p. 527-531

87   "Jeanie Wishart of Pitarrow came of the family of the Earls of
     Argyll who played such a big role in the history of Scotland... The
     younger branch of the family, to which Jeanie Wishart of Pitarrow
     belonged—she was the fifth child of George Wishart, an Edinburgh
     minister—also produced a number of prominent men. William
     Wishart, Jenny's great-grandfather, accompanied the Prince of
     Orange to England, and his brother was the celebrated Admiral
     James Wishart. Jenny's grandmother, Anne Campbell of Orchard,
     wife of the minister, belonged to the old Scottish aristocracy too."

Boris Nicolaievsky and Otto Maenchen-Helfen, *Karl Marx: Man and Fighter* (London: Methuen & Co. Ltd., 1936), pp 21-22; "Baron Ludwig von Westphalen, a senior official of the Royal Prussian Provincial Government, was a man of doubly aristocratic lineage: his father had been Chief of the General Staff during the Seven Years' War and his Scottish mother, Anne Wishart, was descended from the Earls of Argyll." Francis Wheen, *Karl Marx: A Life* (New York and London: W.W. Norton & Company, 1999), page 18

88   "The Communist League, which was the organized expression of the movement, was an international secret society with its headquarters in London. ... The headquarters of the movement, in 1847, were in London, where an Arbeiter Bildungsverein—Workingmen's Educational Club—had existed for seven years. The London Communistische Arbeiter Bildungsverein was founded in February, 1840, by three German exiles ... . The organization prospered and, because of its rather unusual prosperity and stability, and the fact that there was much greater freedom in London than on the Continent, it became, naturally, the central organization." John Spargo, *Karl Marx: His Life and Work* (New York: B.W. Huebsch, 1912), pp 93-94

89   Franz Mehring, *Karl Marx: The Story of His Life*, translated by Edward Fitzgerald (London: George Allin & Unwin Ltd, 1936), page 243-244

90   Gertrude Robinson, *David Urquhart: Some Chapters in the Life of a Victorian Knight-Errant of Justice and Liberty* (Boston and New York: Houghton Mifflin Co., 1920), pp 22, 320

91   Robinson, *David Urquhart* (1920), pp 12-15

92   Spargo (1912), pp 198-199; Mehring (1936), page 244

93 Francis Wheen, *Karl Marx: A Life* (New York and London: W.W. Norton & Company, 1999), pp 207-213

94 Wheen (1999), page 212

95 Spargo (1912), page 198

96 David Urquhart, *Wealth and Want* (London: John Ollivier, 1845), page 14-17

97 Spargo (1912), page 198

98 Urquhart (1845), pp 14-17

99 "Mr W. B. Ferrand, on the other hand, a Yorkshire squire, and John Manners' colleague and life-long friend, boldly attributed all the miseries of England to the greed and selfishness of the manufacturers. His eagle eye detected an immoral alliance between the Poor Law and the factory system. There was a deep-laid design, he was sure, concocted between the wealthy cotton-spinners and the Poor Law Commissioners to undo the country. The proprietors of large estates, he declared, set the very best example by their conduct toward the suffering poor, while the manufacturers made vast fortunes by the sweat of their labourers. In a speech which he made in 1842 ... he pictured the working men and women receiving money-payment for their wages in one room, and then driven into another in which they were compelled to spend every farthing in the purchase of food and clothing. ... The Chartists made a third party to the quarrel. ... They had the sense to perceive that the [Anti-Corn-Law] League was supported by the omnipotent middle-class, and that cheap bread meant low wages. ... Lord John, meanwhile, was doing his best to advocate a happier, more humane life for the people ... '[T]he mists are rolling away [Manners wrote in 1842] and the alternaitve will soon present itself—a democracy or a

Feudalism.' Thus he comes back always to a simple faith in a restored feudalism. … 'Let us show the people, i.e. the lower orders … that we are their real friends … In a word, let society take a more feudal appearance that it presents now.' [Manners wrote in 1842]." Charles Whibley, *Lord John Manners and His Friends* (Edinburgh and London: William Blackwood and Sons, 1925), pp 121-123, 136-137

100 Rutland, John James Robert Manners, 7th Duke of (1818- _____), *Encyclopedia Britannica, Volume 32*, (Edinburgh and London, Adam & Charles Black, 1902), pp 352-353

101 Whibley (1925), pp 121-125; [Arnold Toynbee, 1884] "Now, who really initiated these movements, and who opposed them? Robert Owen was the founder of co-operation … Again, who passed the factory legislation? Not the Radicals; it was due to Owen, Oastler, Sadler, Fielden, and Lord Shaftesbury, to Tory-Socialists and to landowners. And let us recognise the fact plainly, that it is because there has been a ruling aristocracy in England that we have had a great Socialist programme carried out." Arnold Toynbee, *Lectures on the Industrial Revolution in England* (London: Rivingtons, 1884), p 214; [Joseph Rayner Stephens, 1868] "You know what a hard, up-hill battle we have had to fight, and after what fearful opposition at last we won the day. But we did win it; and by whose help did we bring the struggle to a peaceful issue? I need hardly tell you. With the exception of a few noble-hearted men in the ranks of Radicalism such as Fielden, Brotherton, Hindley, and one or two more—our patrons and co-adjutors were found amongst the Tories. When we wanted help, it was not to Cobden and Bright and the political economists that we went to seek it. It was to the 'bloated' aristocrat, to the much-maligned clergyman and country gentleman that we

made our appeal, and from them that we obtained active assistance and influential patronage." Joseph Rayner Stephens, *The Altar, the Throne, and the Cottage: A Speech* (Stalybridge: John Macleod, 1868), page 9.

102 Whibley (1925), pp 133-135

103 Whibley (1925), pp 134-135

104 Karl Marx and Frederick Engels, *The Communist Manifesto* (Chicago: Charles H. Kerr & Company, 1906), page 34

105 "Statement of Hon. Daniel F. Cohalan, Justice of the Supreme Court of New York," (August 30, 1919), United States Senate, Committee on Foreign Relations, Hearings on the Treaty of Peace with Germany (First Session), Sixty-Sixth Congress (Washington: Government Printing Office, 1919), pp 761, 768

106 Cohalan, US Senate, August 30, 1919, page 761

107 Cohalan, US Senate, August 30, 1919, page 770

108 Cohalan, US Senate, August 30, 1919, page 770

109 Karl Marx and Frederick Engels, *The Communist Manifesto* (Chicago: Charles H. Kerr & Company, 1906), p16

110 Carroll Quigley, *Tragedy and Hope: A History of the World in Our Time* (New York: The Macmillan Company, 1966), pp 130-134

111 "Kerensky on Allied Intrigues," *Soviet Russia: Official Organ of the Russian Soviet Government Bureau, Vol. II* (New York, The Russian Soviet Government Bureau, January-June, 1920), page 619

112 Quigley (1966), pp 130-134

113 "A View of Socialism by the Late Viscount Milner," *The National Review*, No. 575, January 1931, pp 36-58

114 Arnold Toynbee, *Lectures on the Industrial Revolution in England* (London: Rivingtons, 1884), page 213

115 Toynbee (1884), page 214

116 Viscount Alfred Milner, "German Socialists," lecture at Whitechapel, 1882; published posthumously in *The National Review*, No. 578, April 1931, pp 477-499

117 Milner, "German Socialists" (1882), pp 477-499

118 "A View of Socialism by the Late Viscount Milner," *The National Review*, No. 575, January 1931, pp 36-58

119 Milner, "German Socialists" (1882), pp477-499

120 "Czar's Stubbornness Caused his Downfall: Refused to Listen to British Statesman Who was Sent to Advise Him," *Evening Star* (Washington, DC), March 16, 1917

121 P.A. Lockwood, "Milner's Entry into the War Cabinet, December 1916," *The Historical Journal*, VII, I, (1964), page 123

122 Sir George Buchanan, *My Mission to Russia, Vol. 2* (1923), page 52; *The Great War: The Standard History of the All-Europe Conflict, Vol. 9*, editors H.W. Wilson, J.A. Hammerton (London, The Amalgamated Press Ltd, 1917), page 117

123 *The Great War: The Standard History of the All-Europe Conflict, Vol. 9*, editors H.W. Wilson, J.A. Hammerton (London, The Amalgamated Press Ltd, 1917) pp 121-122

124 "On January 29 the Allied delegates arrived, and a preliminary meeting was held in the afternoon under the presidency of the Foreign Minister, Pokrowski. Great Britain was represented by Lord Milner, Lord Revelstoke, General Sir Henry Wilson and myself..." Sir George Buchanan, *My Mission to Russia and Other Diplomatic Memories, Vol. 2* (London, Cassell and Company, Ltd, 1923), page 52; "On February 27th, 1917, the Conference of the Allies at

Petrograd... came to an end, and the chief British representative, Lord Milner, left for England in a troubled frame of mind." *The Great War: The Standard History of the All-Europe Conflict, Vol. 9*, editors H.W. Wilson, J.A. Hammerton (London, The Amalgamated Press Ltd, 1917), page 117

125 "Revolution in Russia: Progress of Revolt," *The Daily Telegraph* (London), March 17, 1917, page 7

126 Maurice Paléologue, *An Ambassador's Memoirs: Last French Ambassador to the Russian Court (Volume III, August 19, 1916-May 17, 1917)*, trans. F.A. Holt, O.B.E., (London, Hutchinson & Co., 1925), p 232

127 "Revolution in Russia: Progress of Revolt," *The Daily Telegraph* (London), March 17, 1917, page 7

128 Paléologue (1925), page 167

129 Buchanan (1923), pp 67-71

130 Mark D. Steinberg and Vladimir M. Khrustalev (eds), *The Fall of the Romanovs* (Yale University Press, 1995), page 91; *Romanov Autumn: Stories from the Last Century of Imperial Russia*, page 342; "Tsuyoshi Hasegawa, Rodzianko and the Grand Dukes' Manifesto of 1 March 1917," Canadian Slavonic Papers/Revue Canadienne des Slavistes, Vol. 18, No. 2 (June 1976), pp 154-167

131 Buchanan (1923), page 68

132 Buchanan (1923), page 68

133 Buchanan (1923), page 68

134 Princess Paley, "Mes Souvenirs de Russie," *Revue de Paris*, June 1, 1922

135 "Sir G. Buchanan Cheered," *The Times* (London), March 16, 1917, page 7

136 "Britain's Envoy is Active Real Power for Entente: Newspaper Correspondent Describes Buchanan as a Dictator," *The Salt Lake Tribune* (Salt Lake City), March 25, 1917, page 17

137 "An Attempt to Avert Revolution: Lord Milner's Mission," *The Guardian* (London), March 16, 1917, page 5

138 Parliamentary Debates (Hansard). House of Commons official report, Volume 91, By Great Britain. Parliament. House of Commons, 1917, page 1938

139 "Lord Milner and the Rebellion," *The North Star* (Durham, England), March 23, 1917, page 1; Parliamentary Debates. House of Commons, March 22, 1917, Vol 91, Col 2093

140 *The Times History of the War, Volume XIII* (London: *The Times*, 1917), page 108

141 Parliamentary Debates (Hansard). House of Commons official report, Volume 91, By Great Britain. Parliament. House of Commons, 1917, page 2087

142 "Foreign Policy: 'All Rumours of a Separate Peace Must Vanish'," *Evening Standard* (London), March 24, 1917, page 2

143 Buchanan (1923), page 99

144 Buchanan (1923), pp 113-114

145 Prit Buttar, *Russia's Last Gasp: The Eastern Front 1916-17* (Oxford: Osprey Publishing, 2017), pp 138–155

146 Buchanan (1923), page 114

147 Buchanan (1923), pp 179-181

148 Buchanan (1923), page 166

149 Buchanan (1923), page 173

150 Alexander F. Kerensky, *The Catastrophe: Kerensky's Own Story of*

the Russian Revolution (New York and London: D. Appleton and Company, 1927) p 315

151 "Oliver Locker-Lampson had gone to Russia with a British armoured-car squadron, whcih had been sent as a gesture of Allied solidarity in the fight against Germany, and had been wounded. This eccentric but admittedly brave man involved himself in political intrigues from the moment he arrived in the country, even to the extent of, so he claimed, being invited to help to murder Rasputin. It was not surprising, therefore, that the commander-in-chief of the Russian army, a tough Cossack called Lavr Kornilov, strongly urged Locker-Lampson to help him stage a counter-revolution. Locker-Lampson agreed, and plans were finalised. The British Ambassador, Sir George Buchanan, knew about the plot, did nothing to stop it, and got himself well out of the way by arranging to spend the day on the British residents' golf course." Philip Knightley, *The First Casualty: The War Correspondent as Hero and Myth-Maker from the Crimea to Iraq* (Baltimore and London: The Johns Hopkins University Press, 2004), p 156; "[When] Kornilov ordered the troops under his command to march on the capital to unseat the government, one of the few units which proved faithful to him was a British armoured-car squadron, under Commander Oliver Locker-Lampson, whose members were furnished with Russian uniforms for the occasion. Warth speculates that Knox arranged for their participation ... " Richard Henry Ullman, *Anglo-Soviet Relations, 1917-1921, Volume 2: Britain and the Russian Civil War*, (Princeton, NJ: Princeton University Press, 1961), pp 11-12; "They hoped that I would assist them by placing the British armoured cars at their disposal and by helping them to

escape should their enterprise fail. I replied that it was a very naïve proceeding on the part of those gentlemen to ask an Ambassador to conspire against the Government to which he was accredited and that if I did my duty I ought to denounce their plot. Though I would not betray their confidence, I would not give them either my countenance or support. I would, on the contrary, urge them to renounce an enterprise that was not only foredoomed to failure, but that would at once be exploited by the Bolsheviks. If General Korniloff were wise he would wait for the Bolsheviks to make the first move and then come and put them down." Buchanan (1923), p 175-176

152 Leonard Schapiro, *The Origin of the Communist Autocracy: Political Opposition in the Soviet State, First Phase 1917-1922*, (London: Macmillan/Palgrave, 1977), page 52

153 Joseph Stalin, "The October Revolution," *Pravda*, No. 241, November 6, 1918, cited in Joseph Stalin, *The October Revolution* (Moscow, 1934), page 30

154 Steve R. Dunn, *Battle in the Baltic: The Royal Navy and the Fight to Save Estonia & Latvia 1918-1920* (Barnsley, UK: Seaforth Publishing, 2020), page 34

155 Gilbert (1990), page 229

156 Gilbert (1990), pp 227-230: "By the end of December 1918 there were more than 180,000 non-Russian troops within the frontiers of the former Russian Empire, among them British, American, Japanese, French, Czech, Serb, Greek, and Italian. Looking to these troops from military and moral support, and depending on them for money and guns, were several anti-Bolshevik armies of 'White' Russians, amounting to over 300,000 men. On every front,

the Bolsheviks were being pressed back towards Moscow." (page 227) "On December 31, 1918 Lloyd George invited Churchill to attend a meeting of the Imperial War Cabinet ... (page 228) ...The minutes of the meeting recorded [Lloyd George saying] ... "The Bolsheviks had raised their forces to 300,000, which might exceed 1,000,000 by March, and had greatly improved their organisation." (pp 229-230)

157 Princess Paley, *Memories of Russia 1916-1919* (London, Herbert Jenkins Limited, 1924), pp 41-42

158 "England's policy has always been the dismemberment of Russia. It was for this reason that it supplied with arms, ammunition, officers, money and advice such counter-revolutionary leaders as Denikin and Koltchak. ... Britain wished to divide and then be the patron and protector of the parts." Louis Fischer, *Oil Imperialism: The International Struggle for Petroleum* (New York: International Publishers, 1926), p 32; "There is a possibility that he [Lloyd George] hoped for the ultimate division of Russia into a number of independent states, each too small to cause trouble." Robert W. Sellen, "The British Intervention in Russia, 1917-1920," *Dalhousie Review*, Volume 40 (1960-61), page 525; Gilbert (1990), pp 234-235, 228-229; "Without Russia, Alfred Milner feared, the Allies might not be able to defeat Germany. And the spread of revolution could prove a more dangerous enemy to the established order than the Germans. Why, he wondered, should Britain and France not settle their differences with the Germans—and then partition Russia among themselves? Britain's share, it hardly need be said, would include the central Asian parts of the Russian Empire that adjoined Persia and Afghanistan, strategic borderlands to India. If Germany were willing—and, also

willing, of course to withdraw from France and Belgium—there were many interesting ways in which Russia could be divided. For a full year to come, Milner quietly but doggedly promoted this idea. There is no clear evidence that he or anyone else ever approached the Germans and his proposal apparently never moved beyond the realm of confidential talk within the British government, but it bears a strange resemblance to the world of abruptly shifting superpower alliances that George Orwell would later imagine in 1984." Adam Hochschild, *To End All Wars: A Story of Loyalty and Rebellion 1914-1918* (New York: Houghton Mifflin Harcourt, 2011), pp. 293–294; "Churchill again envisaged a compromise peace ... in which the Bolsheviks would accept the permanent existence of a non-Bolshevik South Russia, with Kiev as its capital, and the Black Sea as its southern frontier. Once a secure dividing line were reached, Britain could sponsor negotiations between Lenin and Denikin." Gilbert (1990), page 329

159 Gilbert, *World in Torment* (1990), pp 288, 291, 296-297, 306-309
160 Gilbert, *World in Torment* (1990), pp 241, 254
161 Nearly 60,000 British troops served in the Russian Civil War, most in the oil-rich Caucasus (40,000), a lesser number in North Russia (14,378), with smaller numbers in Siberia (1,800), Trans-Caspia (950), and elsewhere. "By January 1919... the British presence in the Caucasus totalled 40,000, the largest of all British intervention contingents in Russia." Timothy C. Winegard, *The First World Oil War* (Toronto: University of Toronto Press, 2016), p. 229; For British troop strength on other fronts, see the following: Clifford Kinvig, *Churchill's Crusade: The British Invasion of Russia 1918–1920* (London: Hambledon Continuum, 2006), page 35; Michael Sargent, *British*

Military Involvement in Transcaspia: 1918–1919 (Camberley: Conflict Studies Research Centre, Defence Academy of the United Kingdom, April 2004), page 33; Damien Wright, *Churchill's Secret War with Lenin: British and Commonwealth Military Intervention in the Russian Civil War, 1918-20* (Solihull, UK: Helion & Company Limited, 2017), pp 305-306, 394, 526-528, 530-535

162 [See footnote 158 for additional sources on British plans to break up the Russian Empire.] "Churchill wrote to Lloyd George on 17 June 1918: … 'It we cannot reconstitute the fighting front against Germany in the East, no end can be discerned to the war. Vain will be all sacrifices of the peoples and the armies.'" (page 221) "Lloyd George was opposed to using Allied troops to destroy Bolshevism, or to force the Russians to negotiate with each other. The farthest he was prepared to go was to help those border States in the Baltic and the Caucasus which were struggling to be independent from Russia, and which contained non-Russian majorities." (page 229) "On January 13 [1919], the Imperial War Cabinet met in Paris, with Lloyd George in the chair, to discuss future action in Russia. Sir Henry Wilson, who was present, wrote in his diary: 'It was quite clear that the meeting favoured no troops being sent to fight Bolshevists but on the other hand to help those States which we considered were Independent States by giving them arms, etc.'" (p 234). Martin Gilbert, *World in Torment* (1990), pp 221, 229, 234; [Churchill speech, February 15, 1920] "Now Russia is no longer available. She is no longer the great counterpoise to Germany. On the contrary, she is very likely to go over to the other side, very likely to fall into the hands of the Germans and make a common policy with them. Our interest has been to try to secure a Government in

Russia which will not throw itself into the hands of Germany. ... It is also in our interest not to drive Germany into the arms of Russia." "Mr. Churchill on Bolshevism," *The Times* (London), February 16, 1920, page 7

163 Richard H. Ullman, *Anglo-Soviet Relations, 1917-1921, Volume I: Intervention and the War* (London: Oxford University Press, 1961), pp 116-119

164 Ullman (1961), pp 116-119

165 Ullman (1961), pp 116-119

166 Damien Wright, *Churchill's Secret War with Lenin: British and Commonwealth Military Intervention in the Russian Civil War, 1918-20* (Solihull, UK: Helion & Company Limited, 2017), page 21

167 Wright (2017), page 21

168 Wright (2017), page 22

169 Wright (2017), pp 23-25

170 Martin Gilbert, *World in Torment: Winston S. Churchill 1917-1922* (London: Minerva, 1990; originally 1975 by William Heinemann Ltd), pp 228-22

171 Gilbert (1990), page 234

172 Gilbert (1990), pp 234-235

173 Gilbert (1990), page 288

174 Gilbert (1990), page 291

175 "On June 4 Kolchak replied to an Allied note of May 26, refusing the Allied demand to summon the Constituent Assembly of 1917, and giving an evasive answer about the future sovereignty of Finland and the Baltic States, both of which had been Russian before the revolution. ... [D]espite Kolchak's refusal to accept the Allies' democratic demands, both Churchill and his War Office advisers

continued with the Kotlas plan to link Kolchak's forces with those in North Russia." Gilbert (1990), pp 296-297; Jonathan Smele, *The "Russian" Civil Wars, 1916–1926* (Oxford: Oxford University Press, 2017), pp 111–112

176 Gilbert (1990), pp 306-309

177 Gilbert (1990), pp 306

178 Gilbert (1990), pp 306-309

179 Gilbert (1990), page 224

180 Gilbert (1990), pp 307-308

181 Erick Trickey, "The Forgotten Story of the American Troops Who Got Caught Up in the Russian Civil War," *Smithsonian Magazine* [online], February 12, 2019: https://www.smithsonianmag.com/history/forgotten-doughboys-who-died-fighting-russian-civil-war-180971470

182 Ibid.

183 Ibid.

184 "The last British troops left Archangel on September 27, 1919, and Murmansk on October 12, sealing the fate of North Russia. ...The British mission in Siberia was abolished in March, 1920. ...The tiny British force at Batum was finally withdrawn in July, 1920." Robert W. Sellen, "The British Intervention in Russia, 1917-1920," *Dalhousie Review*, Volume 40 (1960-61), pp 524, 527

185 Gilbert (1990), page 362

186 Boris Egorov, "How a French General Betrayed the Supreme Ruler of Russia," *Russia Beyond*, August 16, 2021: https://www.rbth.com/history/334103-how-french-general-betrayed-kolchak

187 P.J. Gapelotti, *Our Man in the Crimea: Commander Hugo Koehler and the Russian Civil War* (Columbia, SC: University of South Carolina Press, 1991), page 168

188   David Renton, *Trotsky* (London: Haus Publishing, 2004), page 143

189   Pavel Sudoplatov and Anatoli Sudoplatov, *Special Tasks: The Memoirs of an Unwanted Witness—A Soviet Spymaster* (New York: Little, Brown & Company, 1994), page 65-86; Enrique Soto-Pérez-de-Celis, "The Death of Leon Trotsky," *Neurosurgery*, Volume 67 Number 2, August 1, 2010, pp 417–423

190   "The rumour spread that they were having an affair. Although she did not confirm this in her memoir she gave a lot of tactile details which in inter-war Britain fell only just inside the boundaries of the seemly—and the liaison would be brought up by Natalya against Trotsky when they had a serious marital rift in Mexico. The rest of his entourage in the 1930s shared the suspicion about the relationship with Sheridan. Nothing was ever proved; and if an affair took place it was a brief one. In mid-1920, when he had to rejoin the Red Army on its Polish campaign, Trotsky invited her to go along with him on his train but she refused. Instead she left for England, published her diary and went on a publicity tour of America." Robert Service, *Trotsky*: A Biography (Cambridge, MA: Belknap Press, 2009), page 266

191   "In July 1918 the *Committee on Russian Affairs* was formed under the patronage and direction of the former British Ambassador to Russia, George Buchanan. The Committee had the support of Britain's most resourceful wartime propaganda specialists: Sir Bernard Pares, John Buchan, Harold Williams and Hugh Walpole—the very men who had formed the backbone of the British Russian Bureau that had worked so closely and so diligently alongside Military Intelligence in Petrograd during the war. Shortly after their formation, the British War Cabinet requested that a White Paper be drawn up that would

give a blow by blow account of the Bolshevik abuses being carried out in Russia. … The report, which would eventually become known as the Russia No. 1 White Paper (April 1919)—and more informally as the 'Bolshevik Atrocity Blue Book'—made frantic efforts to portray Lenin's Bolsheviks as power-hungry Jewish radicals out to unleash their venom and frustration on the capitalist world at large." Sarjeant, *The Protocols Matrix* (2021), pp 26-27

192   Further Vote on Account,. HC Deb 05 November 1919 vol 120 cc1535-645; cited in The Cause of World Unrest, page 2: https://api.parliament.uk/historic-hansard/commons/1919/nov/05/further-vote-on-account

193   Erich von Ludendorff, *Ludendorff's Own Story, Volume II* (New York and London: Harper & Brothers Publishers, 1919), page 126

194   Leon Trotsky, *My Life: An Attempt at an Autobiography* (Harmondsworth, Middlesex: Penguin.1975), page 172

195   John T. Flynn, "The Merchant of Death: Basil Zakharoff," Mises Daily (online), December 24, 2021 https://mises.org/mises-daily/merchant-death-basil-zaharoff [accessed April 7, 2024]

196   "Sir Basil Zaharoff," britannica.com [accessed April 29, 2024]

197   Z. A. B. Zeman and W. B. Scharlau, *The Merchant of Revolution: The Life of Alexander Israel Helphand (Parvus) 1867-1924* (London: Oxford University Press, 1965), page 152

198   Jim MacGregor and Gerry Docherty, *Prolonging the Agony: How the Anglo-American Establishment Deliberately Extended WWI by Three-and-a-Half Years* (Chicago: Independent Publishers Group, 2017), page 457

199   *Boche and Bolshevik: Being a Series of Articles from the Morning Post of London*, written by Mrs. Nesta Webster and Herr Kurt Kerlen (New York: The Beckwith Company, 1923), pp 24-25

200 Guido Giacomo Preparata, *Conjuring Hitler: How Britain and America Made the Third Reich* (London: Pluto Press, 2005), pp 30-31

201 Z. A. B. Zeman and W. B. Scharlau, *The Merchant of Revolution: The Life of Alexander Israel Helphand (Parvus) 1867-1924* (London: Oxford University Press, 1965), pp 151-152

202 Zeman and Scharlau (1965), pp 150-153

203 Zeman and Scharlau (1965), page 152

204 Preparata (2005), page 32

205 Mrs. Nesta Webster and Herr Kurt Kerlen, *Boche and Bolshevik: Being a Series of Articles from the Morning Post of London* (New York City: The Beckwith Company, 1923), pp 18-19

206 Winston Churchill, "Zionism versus Bolshevism," *Illustrated Sunday Herald*, February 8, 1920, page 5: https://archive. org/details/WinstonChurchillZionismVsBolshevismStruggle ForTheSoulOfTheJewishPeople1920

207 "Freemasonry," *The Holocaust Encyclopedia* (online): https:// encyclopedia.ushmm.org/content/en/article/freemasonry [accessed April 23, 2024]

208 "Freemasonry," *The Holocaust Encyclopedia* (online): https:// encyclopedia.ushmm.org/content/en/article/freemasonry [accessed April 23, 2024]

209 Winston Churchill, "Zionism versus Bolshevism," *Illustrated Sunday Herald*, February 8, 1920, page 5: https://archive.org/details/ WinstonChurchillZionismVsBolshevismStruggleForTheSoul OfTheJewishPeople1920

210 Nesta Webster, *Spacious Days: An Autobiography* (London: Hutchinson & Co., 1950), pp 11-12

211 "Edwyn Bevan, then the most prominent classicist, from

Oxford University, was placed in charge of liaison with the offices of military and naval intelligence... All the men in the above group served as the decision-making body of Wellington House which met several times a week and was known as 'the Moot'." Gary S. Messinger, *British Propaganda and the State in the First World War* (Manchester, UK: Manchester University Press, 1992), page 39

212 Proceedings of the British Academy, Volume 29, 1943, page 416

213 Nesta H. Webster, *The French Revolution: A Study in Democracy* (London: Constable and Company, Ltd., 1920), page 20

214 Webster (1920), page 21

215 Nesta H. Webster, *World Revolution: The Plot Against Civilization* (Boston: Small, Maynard & Company, 1921), page 93

216 Nesta Webster, "The Hidden Hand of Germany—Throwing Dust in the Allies' Eyes," April 26, 1922, cited in *Boche and Bolshevik: Being a Series of Articles from the Morning Post of London*, written by Mrs. Nesta Webster and Herr Kurt Kerlen (New York: The Beckwith Company, 1923), pp 1-2

217 Norman Cohn, *Warrant for Genocide: They Myth of the Jewish World Conspiracy and the Protocols of the Elders of Zion* (London: Serif, 1996), page 31

218 Dilworth, Mark. "Horn, Alexander (1762–1820)," *Oxford Dictionary of National Biography*, Oxford University Press, 2004

219 Edmund Burke to Abbé Barruel, May 1, 1797, in Thomas W. Copeland, ed., *The Correspondence of Edmund Burke, 10 Vols.* (Chicago and Cambridge, 1958–1978), 9: 319–320

220 Edmund Burke to Abbé Barruel, May 1, 1797

221 John Robison, *Proofs of a Conspiracy against all the Religions and*

Governments of Europe, carried on in the secret meetings of Freemasons, Illuminati and Reading Societies (Edinburgh: Printed for William Creech; and T. Cadell, junior, and W. Davies, London, 1797)

222 Norman Cohn, *Warrant for Genocide: They Myth of the Jewish World Conspiracy and the Protocols of the Elders of Zion* (London: Serif, 1996), pp 31-36

223 Cohn (1996), pp 32-33

224 Cohn (1996), page 36; Claus Oberhauser, "Simonini's letter: the 19th century text that influenced antisemitic conspiracy theories about the Illuminati," The Conversation (online), March 31, 2020: https://theconversation.com/simoninis-letter-the-19th-century-text-that-influenced-antisemitic-conspiracy-theories-about-the-illuminati-134635 [accessed March 31, 2024]

225 Charles Whibley, *Lord John Manners and His Friends* (Edinburgh and London: William Blackwood and Sons, 1925), 84-85, 147, 149, 174, 188, 309-310

226 B. Disraeli Esq. M.P., Coningsby; or The New Generation, Vol. II (London: Henry Colburn, 1844), page 126

227 Disraeli (1844), page 201

228 Dr. Stanley Monteith, *Brotherhood of Darkness* (Oklahoma City, OK: Hearthstone Publishing, 2000), page 36

229 Nesta H. Webster, *World Revolution: The Plot Against Civilization* (Boston: Small, Maynard & Company, 1921), page 307

230 Webster (1921), page 308

231 "Most accounts of the development of Marx's economic ideas emphasise the dual contributions of classical political economy and Hegelian philosophy ... The early English radical economists, known collectively (but inappropriately) as the Ricardian Socialists, are

generally dismissed as incoherent utopians, or ignored. This article suggests, on the contrary, that they constituted a third-important though very largely neglected-influence on Marx's thought. Esther Lowenthal's classic book of 1911, *The Ricardian Socialists*... restricted itself to just four men: John Francis Bray, John Gray, Thomas Hodgskin, and William Thompson. ... For the purposes of the present article ... [an] earlier writer of 1805, Charles Hall, will also be included ... the Ricardian Socialists were closer to 'the revelation of the secret of capitalistic production through surplus value' than Engels allowed. ... some of them were on the verge of elaborating a 'materialistic conception of history' not entirely dissimilar to Marx's own." J.E. King, "Utopian or Scientific? A Reconsideration of the Ricardian Socialists," *History of Political Economy*, Volume 14, Issue 3, Fall 1983, pp 345-373

232 "In September, 1864, the International Workingmen's Association was founded, and Marx at once became its acknowledged, but unofficial, leader. For the next seven years his life was mainly devoted to the affairs of that greatest proletarian organization of modern times, so that to write the story of the International is to write the life of its founder during that period." Spargo (1912), page 227

233 F.M. Leventhal, *Respectable Radical: George Howell and Victorian Working Class Politics* (London: Weidenfeld and Nicolson, 1971), pp 50-52

234 Rolf Hosfeld, *Karl Marx: An Intellectual Biography* (Oxford, New York: Berghahn Books, 2012), pp 105-106

235 Anton Chaitkin, *Treason in America: From Aaron Burr to Averell Harriman* (Washington, DC: Executive Intelligence Review, 1998), pp 124, 129-134, 138, 146, 157, 160, 189, 190, 195, 198, 466-467, 527

236 Richard Poe, "How the British Caused the American Civil War," Substack.com, December 30, 2021: https://richardpoe. substack.com/p/how-the-british-caused-the-american?utm_ source=profile&utm_medium=reader2 [accessed May 3, 2024]

237 Spargo (1912) pp 228-229

238 Krzysztof Marchlewicz, "For Independent Poland and the Emancipation of the Working Class" pp 181-192, in *"Arise Ye Wretched of the Earth": The First International in a Global Perspective*, edited by Fabrice Bensimon, Quentin Deluermoz, and Jeanne Moisand (Leiden, Boston: Brill, 2018)

239 Speech delivered in London, probably to a meeting of the International's General Council and the Polish Workers Society on 22 January 1867, text published in *Le Socialisme*, 15 March 1908; Odbudowa Polski (Warsaw, 1910), pp. 119–23; Mysl Socjalistyczna, May 1908. From Karl Marx and Frederick Engels, *The Russian Menace to Europe*, edited by Paul Blackstock and Bert Hoselitz (London: George Allen and Unwin, 1953), pp 104–08.

240 Spargo (1912), page 280

241 Spargo (1912), page 219

242 Max Beer, *The Life and Teaching of Karl Marx*, translated by T.C. Partington and H.J. Stenning (London: National Labour Press, Limited, 1921), page 59

243 Beer (1921), page 60

244 Marx to Domela Nieuwenhuis in The Hague, London, February 22, 1881: https://www.marxists.org/archive/marx/works/1881/ letters/81_02_22.htm

245 Spargo (1912), page 294

246 Spargo (1912), pp 296-297

247 Spargo (1912), page 60

248 "A View of Socialism by the Late Viscount Milner," *The National Review*, No. 575, January 1931, pp 36-58

249 Nesta H. Webster, *World Revolution: The Plot Against Civilization* (Boston: Small, Maynard & Company, 1921), page 315

250 Nesta H. Webster, "A Deep-Laid Conspiracy—The Deutsche Bank and Communism," April 27, 1922, cited in *Boche and Bolshevik: Being a Series of Articles from the Morning Post of London*, written by Mrs. Nesta Webster and Herr Kurt Kerlen (New York: The Beckwith Company, 1923), Page 11

251 Sharman Kadish, *Bolsheviks and British Jews: The Anglo-Jewish Community, Britain and the Russian Revolution* (Abingdon, UK: Taylor & Francis: 2013), pp 36

252 André Chéradame, The Mystification of the Allied Peoples. Why? How? By Whom? (Evreux, France: Ch. Hérissey Press, 1923), trans. John A. FitzGerald, page 248; cited in Nesta Webster, World Revolution

253 Webster (1921), pp 91-92

254 Webster (1921), page 92

255 Webster (1921), pp 92-94

256 Karl Marx, "On the Jewish Question," Autumn 1843: https://www.marxists.org/archive/marx/works/1844/jewish-question

257 George Orwell, *Nineteen Eighty-Four* (New York: New American Library/Signet Classics, 1961), pp 152-153, 246

258 *New York Times*, June 24, 1897; quoted in *National Union Gleanings Vol. IX July-December, 1897* (London: National Union of Conservative and Constitutional Associations; 1897), page 42

259 Alfred Tennyson, *Locksley Hall* (Boston, MA: Ticknor and Fields,

1869), pp 51-53; cited in Dr. Stanley Monteith, *Brotherhood of Darkness* (Oklahoma City, OK: Hearthstone Publishing, 2000), pp 12-13

260 Rt. Hon. Winston Churchill, "Fifty Years Hence," *Maclean's*, November 15, 1931, pp 66-67

261 John Ruskin, *Lectures on Art Delivered Before the University of Oxford in Hilary Term, 1870* (New York: Maynard, Merrill, & Co., 1893), pp 36-37

262 Carroll Quigley, *Tragedy and Hope: A History of the World in Our Time* (New York: The Macmillan Company, 1966), page 130

263 John Ruskin, *Fors Clavigera: Letters to the Workmen and Labourers of Great Britain, Vol. I* (London: George Allen, 1907), page 116

264 Ruskin, 1893, page 35-37; Quigley, 1966, p 130

265 Philip Hoare, "John Ruskin: a Prophet for Our Troubled Times," *New Statesman*, February 13, 2019; Candy Bedworth, "John Ruskin: Painter, Prophet, Pervert," *Daily Art Magazine*, December 3, 2020

266 Quigley (1966, page 130

267 *The Last Will and Testament of Cecil John Rhodes*, edited by W. T. Stead (London, "Review of Reviews" Office: 1902), page 58

268 Basil Williams, *Cecil Rhodes*, (New York, Henry Holt & Company: 1921), page 51

269 Williams (1921, page 51

270 Cecil Rhodes, Confession of Faith, 1877: https://pages.uoregon.edu/kimball/Rhodes-Confession.htm

271 Gerry Docherty and Jim Macgregor, *Hidden History: The Secret Origins of the First World War* (Edinburgh and London: Mainstream Publishing, 2013), pp 71-72

272 Carroll Quigley, *The Anglo-American Establishment: From Rhodes to*

Cliveden (New York: Books in Focus, 1981), pp117-118; Carroll Quigley, *Tragedy and Hope: A History of the World in Our Time* (New York: Macmillan Company, 166), pp 146, 950

273 Quigley (1981), pp117-118; Quigley (1966), page 144

274 Herbert A. Smith, "The British Dominions and Foreign Relations," *The Cornell Law Quarterly*, Vol. XII, No. 1, December 1926, pp1, 4; Quigley, *The Anglo-American Establishment*, 1981, pp117-118, 121; Quigley, *Tragedy and Hope*, 1966, pp 133, 144

275 Quigley (1981), pp 117-118; Quigley (1966), page 144

276 Bradford Perkins, *The Great Rappochement: England and the United States, 1895-1914* (New York: Atheneum Books, 1968), pp 3-11

277 Andrew Carnegie, *The Reunion of Britain and America: A Look Ahead* (Edinburgh: Andrew Elliot, 1893), p 32

278 W.T. Stead, *The Americanization of the World* (New York: Horace Markley, 1901), pp. 396-397

279 Carroll Quigley, The Anglo-American Establishment: From Rhodes to Cliveden (New York: Books in Focus, 1981); Docherty and Macgregor (2013), pp 71-72

280 J.R. Seeley, M.A., *The Expansion of England: Two Courses of Lectures* (Boston: Roberts Brothers, 1883), pp 221-224.

281 Seeley (1883), page 334

282 W.T. Stead, *The Americanization of the World* (New York: Horace Markley, 1901), pp 396-397

283 The Right Hon. Lord Avebury, "The Future of Europe," *The Nineteenth Century and After: A Monthly Review*, Vol. LIX, January-June 1906, pp 416-428.

284 H.G. Wells, "The War That Will End War," *Daily News & Leader*, August 14, 1914

285 H.G. Wells, *The War That Will End War* (London, UK: Frank & Cecil Palmer, October 1914), page 62

286 Peter Edgerly Firchow, *The Death of the German Cousin: Variations on a Literary Stereotype, 1890-1920* (Lewisburg, PA: Bucknell University Press, 1986), p114; Kenneth J. Calder, *Britain and the Origins of the New Europe, 1914-1918* (New York: Cambridge University Press, for the Center of International Studies, London School of Economics and Political Science, 1976), p54; Burton Yale Pines, *America's Greatest Blunder: The Fateful Decision to Enter World War One* (New York: RSD Press, 2013), page 39

287 Charles E. Neu, *Colonel House: A Biography of Woodrow Wilson's Silent Partner* (United States: Oxford University Press, 2014), pp 3-5, 8

288 Godfrey Hodgson, *Woodrow Wilson's Right Hand: The Life of Colonel Edward M. House* (New Haven: Yale University Press, 2006), pp 16-19; Charles E. Neu, *Colonel House: A Biography of Woodrow Wilson's Silent Partner* (United States: Oxford University Press, 2014), pp 3-8.

289 Christopher Andrew, *For the President's Eyes Only: Secret Intelligence and the American Presidency from Washington to Bush* (London: HarperCollins, 1995), p57; Keith Jeffrey, *The Secret History of MI6 1909-1949* (New York: Penguin Press, 2010), page 116

290 Edward Mandell House and Charles Seymour, *The Intimate Papers of Colonel House* (Cambridge, MA: Houghton Mifflin Company, 1926), pp. 87-89, 92

291 Inderjeet Parmar, *Think Tanks and Power in Foreign Policy: A Comparative Study of the Role and Influence of the Council on Foreign Relations and the Royal Institute of International Affairs, 1939-1945* (Basingstoke, UK: Palgrave, 2004), pp 26-27

292 John Bruce Lockhart, "Sir William Wiseman Bart— Agent of Influence," RUSI Journal (Royal United Services Institute for Defense Studies) (Great Britain), vol. 134, no. 2 (Summer 1989), pp 63-67

293 A. J. P. Taylor, Short Notices, *The English Historical Review*, Volume LXXXVI, Issue CCCXXXVIII, January 1971, page 198 (A review of: W.B. Fowler, *British-American Relations, 1917-1918: The Role of Sir William Wiseman* (Princeton, Princeton University Press, 1969)

294 Inderjeet Parmar, *Think Tanks and Power in Foreign Policy: A Comparative Study of the Role and Influence of the Council on Foreign Relations and the Royal Institute of International Affairs, 1939-1945* (Basingstoke, UK: Palgrave, 2004), pp 3, 19, 27, 29, 109

295 Inderjeet Parmar, *Think Tanks and Power in Foreign Policy: A Comparative Study of the Role and Influence of the Council on Foreign Relations and the Royal Institute of International Affairs, 1939-1945* (Basingstoke, UK: Palgrave, 2004), pp 3, 19, 26-27, 29, 109

296 Parmar, *Think Tanks and Power in Foreign Policy*, 2004, pp. 3, 19-20, 26-27, 29

297 Laurence H. Shoup and William Minter, *Imperial Brain Trust: The Council on Foreign Relations and United States Foreign Policy* (New York: Monthly Review Press, 1977), pp 3-7

298 Herb Greer, "Amantium Irae— 'Special' No More: Anglo-American Relations: Rhetoric and Reality by John Dickie," *World Affairs*, Washington, Vol. 157, Issue 2 (Fall 1994): 98

299 See Angell, *The Political Conditions of Allied Success* (New York, 1918); Angel, "The English-Speaking World and the Next Peace," *World Affairs*, 105 (1942), 10; Angell, "The British Commonwealth in the Next World Order." *Annals of the American*

Academy of Political and Social Science, 228 (1943), 65-70; Angell, "Angell Sums Up at 85." *Freedom & Union* (December 1958), 7-11; all cited in Duncan Bell, *Reordering the World: Essays on Liberalism and Empire* (Princeton, NJ: Princeton University Press, October 22, 2019), pp 199-200

300 Sir Winston Spencer Churchill, Harry S. Truman, *The Sinews of Peace: A Speech by Winston Churchill to Westminster College Fulton, Missouri 5 March 1946* (United States: Halcyon-Commonwealth Foundation, 1965)

301 Peter Wilkin, "George Orwell: The English Dissident as Tory Anarchist," *Political Studies*, Vol. 61, Issue 1, March 2013, pp 197-214

302 Alfred Zimmern, *The Third British Empire* (London: Oxford University Press, 1926), page 1

303 Zimmern (1926), page 60

304 H.G. Wells, *Experiment in Autobiography* (Boston: Little, Brown & Co., 1962), pp 650-653

305 Peter Edgerly Firchow, *The Death of the German Cousin: Variations on a Literary Stereotype, 1890-1920* (Lewisburg, PA: Bucknell University Press, 1986), pp 114; Burton Yale Pines, *America's Greatest Blunder: The Fateful Decision to Enter World War One* (New York: RSD Press, 2013), pp 39; Kenneth J. Calder, *Britain and the Origins of the New Eruope, 1914-1918* (New York: Cambridge University Press, for the Centre for International Studies, London School of Economics and Political Science, 1976), page 54

306 H.G. Wells, *Experiment in Autobiography* (Boston: Little, Brown, and Co., 1962), page 652

307 "Britain Putting By Empire for Mankind," *The Boston Globe*, April 23, 1918, page 6

308 "On five of the six occasions he visited London between 1902 and 1911 he made a point of calling into the British Museum…" Bob Henderson, Lenin and the British Museum Library, pages 3-15; in *Solanus: International Journal for Russian & East European Bibliographic, Library & Publishing Studies*, New Series, Vol. 4, 1990 British Museum

309 Alan Sarjeant, "Lenin at 16 Percy Circus, London," Pixel Surgery, November 30, 2011: https://pixelsurgery.wordpress.com/2011/11/30/percy-circus-london/ [accessed May 1, 2024]

310 Ibid.

311 Quigley (1966), page 132

312 Asa Briggs and Anne Macartney, *Toynbee Hall: The First Hundred Years* (London: Routledge & Kegan Paul, 1984), pp 54-55

313 Martin Gilbert, *Winston S. Churchill: Road to Victory 1941-1945, Volume VII* (New York: Houghton-Mifflin, 1986), page 137

314 Gilbert (1986), page 137

315 Sun Yat-sen, *The Vital Problem of China* (Taipei, Taiwan: China Cultural Service, 1953), page 78

316 According to Churchill, his exact words to Stalin were, "So far as Britain and Russia are concerned, how would it do for you to have ninety percent predominance in Romania, for us to have ninety per cent of the say in Greece, and go fifty-fifty about Yugoslavia?" Geoffrey Roberts, *Stalin's Wars: From World War to Cold War, 1939-1953* (New Haven: Yale University Press, 2006), page 218, 406

317 Yuri Modin with Jean-Charles Deniau and Aguieszka Ziarek, translated by Anthony Roberts, *My Five Cambridge Friends: Burgess, MacLean, Philby, Blunt, and Cairncross by their KGB Controller* (New York: Farrar, Strauss, Giroux, 1994), pp 3-4, 109-110, 117-119, 148-149

318   Andy McSmith, "The Fourth Man Speaks: Last Testimony of Anthony Blunt, *Independent*, July 23, 2009: https://www. independent.co.uk/news/people/news/the-fourth-man-speaks-last-testimony-of-anthony-blunt-1757483.html [accessed May 7, 2024]

319   Phillip Knightley, "The Spy Game Was a Con Game," *Baltimore Sun*, October 24, 2018: https://www.baltimoresun.com/1994/11/28/the-spy-game-was-a-con-game/ [accessed May 7, 2024]

320   Dr. Barbara Campbell, "Dr. William Y. Elliott, 82, Dies; A Harvard Professor Emeritus," *The New York Times*, January 11, 1979, Section B, Page 12

321   Stone (2012), page 101

322   Stone (2012), page 22-23

323   "Yet, before America's involvement in World War II even began, Elliott was already cooperating with the Mazzini Society... The Society was coordinating anti-Fascist activity in America... According to Max Corvo, an OSS officer... 'In order... to monitor anti-Fascist activities in the United States, the British relied on their connections with the Mazzini Society.' It would not be surprising if Elliott, the former Rhodes Scholar and friend of the historian/British intelligence agent A.J. Toynbee, was one of their intelligence contacts in America. Toynbee was the director of the Royal Institute of International Affairs when it merged with British Intelligence's Foreign Office in 1939. To securely conduct intelligence gathering and planning, the intelligence apparatus moved to Balliol College, Oxford, whose Master, A.D. Lindsay, had mentored both Toynbee and Elliott. ... As for Elliott's British-backed Mazzini Society, their attempts to regain power in Italy

proved unsuccessful because the Society's 'key men were reported to have contacts with the British intelligence service which was believed to support a post-war retention of the monarchy.'" Stone (2012), pp 63-65

324 Stone (2012), pp 51-52

325 Address by the Honorable Henry A. Kissinger, "Reflections on a Partnership: British and American Attitudes to Postwar Foreign Policy," Royal Institute of International Affairs (Chatham House), London, May 10, 1982, page 8

326 Kissinger, Chatham House (May 10, 1982), page 6

327 Sean Stone, *New World Order: A Strategy of Imperialism* (Walterville, OR: Trine Day LLC), pp 118-119

328 Johnny Vedmore, "Dr. Klaus Schwab or: How the CFR Taught Me to Stop Worrying and Love the Bomb," *Unlimited Hangout*, March 10, 2022: https://unlimitedhangout.com/2022/03/investigative-reports/dr-klaus-schwab-or-how-the-cfr-taught-me-to-stop-worrying-and-love-the-bomb [accessed May 6, 2024]

329 Stone (2012), page 104

330 Vedmore, *Unlimited Hangout*, March 10, 2022

331 Erick Trickey, "The Forgotten Story of the American Troops Who Got Caught Up in the Russian Civil War," *Smithsonian Magazine* [online], February 12, 2019: https://www.smithsonianmag.com/history/forgotten-doughboys-who-died-fighting-russian-civil-war-180971470

332 "The charge of the 21st Lancers at the Battle of Omdurman on Friday, 2 September 1898, was the largest British cavalry charge since the Crimean War forty-four years earlier. Although there were a few afterwards in the Boer War and Great War, it was the last significant

cavalry charge in British history. Churchill, riding 'a handy, sure-footed, grey Arab polo pony', commanded a troop of twenty-five lancers. Many of the Dervishes they attacked were hidden in a dried-out watercourse when the regiment set off, and it was after the charge had begun that the regiment realized they were outnumbered by approximately ten to one." Andrew Roberts, *Churchill: Walking with Destiny* (New York: Penguin Books, 2019), page 57

ABOUT THE AUTHOR

Richard Poe is a *New York Times*-bestselling author and award-winning journalist. He has written many books, on many subjects, both fiction and non-fiction. Poe's best-known book is *The Shadow Party*, an exposé of George Soros and his color revolutions, co-written with David Horowitz. Poe's work can be found at RichardPoe.com, richardpoe.substack.com, and @RealRichardPoe on the X platform.

INDEX

66

6 stop

R

Rakovsky, Christian, 8

Rasputin, Grigory,
   assassinated by British, 12,
      108–109, 209
   leader of peace party in Russian
      court, 108–109, 191

Rayner, Lt. Oswald, 17

Red Army, 3, 7, 90–91, 94, 188,
   216

Red Terror, 85

Revolution,
   Bourgeois revolution, 65–69
   Color revolution, xii, 38–45,
      47, 197, 233
   French Revolution, xiv, 44–46,
      46–50, 51–53, 57, 100,
      112–119, 120–125, 129,
      198, 201, 219
   Russian Revolution, xiv, 3–13,
      17, 23, 30–33, 43–44, 69
   February Revolution, 78–88
   October Revolution, 89–90

Rhodes, Cecil, 151–155, 158,
   161, 167, 171, 224–225, 230

Rhodes, Trust, 151

Robespierre, Maximilien, 47,
   49–50, 199

Robison, John, 117–118,
   120–123, 126, 129, 219

Rodzianko, Mikhail, 10, 78–82,
   207

Romanov,
   Grand Duke Cyril
      Vladimirovich, 78–79
   Grand Duke Dmitri Pavlovich,
      12
   Grand Duke Michael
      Alexandrovich, 79–80
   Grand Duke Nicholas
      Nikolaevich, 27
   Grand Duke Paul
      Alexandrovich, 10, 79
   Prince Vladimir Pavlovich Paley,
      13

Round Table, 149–155, 156–160,
   161, 163, 165, 176–180,
   181–182

Ruskinites, 69, 152, 154,
   170–171

Ruskin, John, 69, 150–152, 154,
   224

Russian Civil War, 3, 6, 12–13,
   90–94, 95–100, 105, 108,
   167, 182, 185–186, 190, 209,
   212–215, 231

Made in United States
Troutdale, OR
12/15/2024